509
SPA
C.1

Spangenburg, Ray,
1939-

The age of
synthesis.

$35.00

34880030013200

DATE			

The History of SCIENCE

THE AGE OF SYNTHESIS

1800–1895

Ray Spangenburg
Diane Kit Moser

Facts On File, Inc.

The Age of Synthesis: 1800–1895

Facts On File, Inc.
132 West 31st Street
New York NY 10001

Library of Congress Cataloging-in-Publication Data

Spangenburg, Ray, 1939–
    The age of synthesis : 1800–1895 / Ray Spangenburg and Diane Kit Moser.
        p. cm. — (History of science series)
    Rev. ed. of: The history of science in the nineteenth century. c1994.
    Summary: Examines the role of science in the Industrial Revolution, its establishment as a popular discipline, and discoveries in the areas of atoms and the elements, chemistry, evolution, and energy.
    Includes bibliographical references and index.
        ISBN 0-8160-4853-3
        1. Science—History—19th century—Juvenile literature. [1. Science—History.] I. Moser, Diane, 1944– II. Spangenburg, Ray, 1939– History of science in the nineteenth century. III. Title.
        Q125.S737 2004
        509.'.034—dc22   2003021409

Facts On File books are available at special discounts when purchased in bulk quantities for businesses, associations, institutions, or sales promotions. Please call our Special Sales Department in New York at (212) 967-8800 or (800) 322-8755.

You can find Facts On File on the World Wide Web at http://www.factsonfile.com

Text design by Erika K. Arroyo
Cover design by Nora Wertz
Illustrations by Jeremy Eagle

Printed in the United States of America

MP Hermitage 10 9 8 7 6 5 4 3 2 1

This book is printed on acid-free paper.

In Memory of
Morgan Sherwood
and his love of the ever–human
struggle to become rational

CONTENTS

PREFACE

What I see in Nature is a magnificent structure that we can comprehend only very imperfectly, and that must fill a thinking person with a feeling of "humility."

—Albert Einstein

SCIENCE, OF ALL HUMAN ENDEAVORS, is one of the greatest adventures: Its job is to explore that "magnificent structure" we call nature and its awesome unknown regions. It probes the great mysteries of the universe such as black holes, star nurseries, and quasars, as well as the perplexities of miniscule subatomic particles, such as quarks and antiquarks. Science seeks to understand the secrets of the human body and the redwood tree and the retrovirus. The realms of its inquiry embrace the entire universe and everything in it, from the smallest speck of dust on a tiny asteroid to the fleck of color in a girl's eye, and from the vast structure of a far-off galaxy millions of light years away to the complex dynamics that keep the rings of Saturn suspended in space.

Some people tend to think that science is a musty, dusty set of facts and statistics to be memorized and soon forgotten. Others contend that science is the antithesis of poetry, magic, and all things human. Both groups have it wrong—nothing could be more growth-oriented or more filled with wonder or more human. Science is constantly evolving, undergoing revolutions, always producing "new words set to the old music," and constantly refocusing what has gone before into fresh, new understanding.

Asking questions and trying to understand how things work are among the most fundamental of human characteristics, and the history of science is the story of how a varied array of individuals,

ix

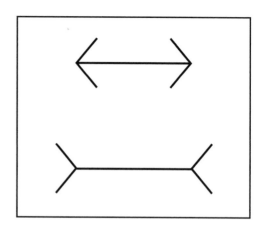

Looks can be deceiving. These two lines are the same length.

teams, and groups have gone about finding answers to some of the most fundamental questions. When, for example, did people begin wondering what Earth is made of and what its shape might be? How could they find answers? What methods did they devise for coming to conclusions and how good were those methods? At what point did their inquiries become *scientific*—and what does that mean?

Science is so much more than the strange test tubes and odd apparatus we see in movies. It goes far beyond frog dissections or the names of plant species that we learn in biology classes. Science is actually a way of thinking, a vital, ever-growing way of looking at the world. It is a way of discovering how the world works—a very particular way that uses a set of rules devised by scientists to help them also discover their own mistakes because it is so easy to misconstrue what one sees or hears or perceives in other ways.

If you find that hard to believe, look at the two horizontal lines in the figure above. One looks like a two-way arrow; the other has inverted arrowheads. Which one do you think is longer (not including the "arrowheads")? Now measure them both. Right, they are exactly the same length. Because it is so easy to go wrong in making observations and drawing conclusions, people developed a system, a "scientific method," for asking "How can I be sure?" If you actually took the time to measure the two lines in our example, instead of just taking our word that both lines are the same length, then you were thinking like a scientist. You were testing your own observation. You were testing the information that both lines "are exactly the same length." And you were employing one of the strongest tools of science to perform your test: You were quantify-ing, or measuring, the lines.

More than 2,300 years ago, Aristotle, a Greek philosopher, told the world that when two objects of different weights were dropped from a height, the heaviest would hit the ground first. It was a com-monsense argument. After all, anyone who wanted to try a test could make an "observation" and see that if you dropped a leaf and a stone together that the stone would land first. Try it yourself with a sheet of notebook paper and a paperweight in your living room. (There is something wrong with this test. Do you know what it is?) However, not many Greek thinkers tried any sort of test. Why bother when the answer was already known? And, since they were philosophers who believed in the power of the human mind to simply "reason" such things out without having to resort to "tests," they considered obser-vation and experiments intellectually and socially beneath them.

Centuries later, though, Galileo Galilei came along, a brilliant Italian pioneer in physics and telescopic astronomy. Galileo liked to figure things out for himself, and he did run some tests, even though he had to work around some limitations. Like today's scientists, Galileo was never content just to watch. He used two balls of differ-ent weights, a time-keeping device, and an inclined plane, or ramp. Accurate clocks and watches were not yet invented, but he worked around that problem by rigging his own device. One at a time, he allowed the balls to roll down the ramp and carefully *measured* the time they took to reach the end of the ramp. He did this not once but many times, inclining planes at many different angles. His results, which still offend the common sense of many people today, indi-cated that, in Aristotle's example, after adjusting for differences in air resistance, all objects released at the same time from the same height would hit the ground at the same time. In a perfect vacuum (which scientists could not create in Galileo's time), all objects would fall at the same rate! You can run a rough test yourself (although it is by no means a really accurate experiment) by crumpling notebook paper into a ball and then dropping it at the same time as the paperweight.

"Wait!" you might justifiably say. Just a minute ago, you dropped a piece of paper and a paperweight and so demonstrated Aristotle's premise when the two objects hit the ground at different times. Now when we do the same thing over again, the two objects hit the ground at about the same time and we demonstrate that Galileo was right and Aristotle was wrong. What makes the difference? You have it: The second time, you crumpled the paper so that it had the same shape as the paperweight. Without crumpling the paper, you would have to make an adjustment for the increased air resistance of an 8½-by-11-inch sheet of paper as opposed to a paperweight that had less surface area.

Galileo's experiments (which he carefully recorded step by step) and his conclusions based on these experiments demonstrate an important attribute of science. Anyone who wanted to could duplicate the experiments and either verify his results or, by showing flaws or errors in the experiments, prove him partially or wholly incorrect. Since his time, many, many scientists have repeated his experiment and, even though they tried, no one ever proved Galileo wrong. There is more. Years later, when it was possible to create a vacuum (even though his experiments had been accurate enough to win everybody over long before that), his prediction proved true. Without any air resistance at all and even with much more sophisticated timing devices, his experiment came out as predicted.

Galileo had not only shown that Aristotle had been wrong. He demonstrated how, by observation, experiment, and quantification, Aristotle, if he had so wished, might have proved himself wrong—and thus changed his own opinion! Above all else the scientific way of thinking is a way to keep yourself from fooling yourself—or from letting nature (or others) fool you.

Of course, science is much more than observation, experimentation, and presentation of results. No one today can read a newspaper or a magazine without becoming quickly aware of the fact that science is always bubbling with "theories." "Astronomer Finds Evidence That Challenges Einstein's Theory of Relativity," announces a magazine cover. "State Board of Education Condemns Books That Teach Darwin's Theory of Evolution," reads a newspaper headline. What is this thing called a "theory"? The answer lies in a process known as the "scientific method."

Few scientists pretend anymore that they have the completely "detached" and objective scientific method proposed by the philosopher Francis Bacon and others at the dawn of the Scientific Revolution in the 17th century. Bacon's method, in its simplest form, proposed that an investigator trying to find out about nature's secrets had an obligation to think objectively and proceed without preformed opinions, basing conclusions on observation, experiments, and collection of data about the phenomena under inquiry. "I make no hypothesis," Isaac Newton announced after demonstrating the universal law of gravity when it was suggested that he might have an idea *what gravity was*. Historians have noted that Newton apparently did have a couple of ideas, or "hypotheses," as to the possible nature of gravity, but for the most part he kept these conjectures private. As far as Newton was concerned, there had already been enough hypothesizing and too little attention paid to the careful gathering of testable facts and figures.

Today, though, we know that scientists may not always follow along the simple and neat pathways laid out by the trail guide known as the "scientific method." Sometimes, either before or after experiments, a scientist will get an idea or a hunch (that is, a somewhat less than well thought out hypothesis) that suggests a new approach or a different way of looking at a problem. Then the researcher will run experiments and gather data to attempt to prove or disprove this hypothesis. Sometimes the word *hypothesis* is used loosely in everyday conversation, but in science it must meet an important requirement: To be valid scientifically a hypothesis must have a built-in way it can be proved wrong if, in fact, it is wrong. That is, it must be falsifiable.

Not all scientists actually run experiments themselves. Most theoreticians, for instance, map out their arguments mathematically. But hypotheses, to be taken seriously by the scientific community, must always carry with them the seeds of falsifiability by experiment and observation.

That brings us to the word *theory*. To become a theory, a hypothesis has to pass several tests. It has to hold up under repeated experiments and not done just by one scientist. Other scientists, working separately from the first, must also perform experiments and observations to test the hypothesis. Then, when thoroughly reinforced by continual testing and appraising, the hypothesis may become known to the scientific and popular world as a "theory."

It is important to remember that even a theory is also subject to falsification or correction. A good theory, for instance, will suggest "predictions"—events that its testers can look for as further tests of its validity. By the time most well-known theories, such as Einstein's theory of relativity or Darwin's theory of evolution, reach the textbook stage, they have survived the gamut of verification to the extent that they have become productive working tools for other scientists. But in science, no theory can be accepted as completely "proved"; it must remain always open to further tests and scrutiny as new facts or observations emerge. It is this insistently self-correcting nature of science that makes it both the most demanding and the most productive of humankind's attempts to understand the workings of nature. This kind of critical thinking is the key element of doing science.

The cartoon-version scientist, portrayed as a bespectacled, rigid man in a white coat and certain of his own infallibility, couldn't be further from reality. Scientists, both men and women, are as human as the rest of us—and they come in all races, sizes, and appearances, with and without eyeglasses. As a group, because their methodology focuses so specifically on fallibility and critical thinking, they are probably even more aware than the rest of us of how easy it is to be wrong. But they like being right whenever possible, and they like working toward finding the right answers to questions. That's usually why they became scientists.

The Age of Synthesis, 1800–1895 and the four other books in The History of Science series look at how people have developed the methods of science as a system for finding out how the world works. We will look at the theories they put forth, sometimes right and sometimes wrong. We will also look at how we have learned to test, accept, and build upon those theories—or to correct, expand, or simplify them.

We will also explore how 19th-century scientists learned from their own and others' mistakes, sometimes having to discard theories—such as phrenology or mesmerism—that once seemed logical but later proved to be incorrect, misleading, or unfruitful. In all these ways these men and women—and the rest of us as well—have built upon the shoulders of men and women of science, the giants, who went before them.

In this edition, each volume in the series contains expanded material, including an increased exploration of the role of women in science; many new photographs and illustrations; an examination of some of the pseudosciences that sprang up in every era in counterpoint to science; and an exploration of the interaction of science and society during the period. Sidebars called "Side Roads of Science" examine weird beliefs and pseudoscientific claims of the times.

Finally, each volume concludes with a glossary, a chronology, and an expanded and updated list of sources for further exploration, including Web sites, CD-ROMs, and other multimedia resources, as well as recent books and other print resources.

ACKNOWLEDGMENTS

WE COULD NOT HAVE WRITTEN this book or the others in this series without the help, inspiration, and guidance offered by many generous individuals over nearly two decades of writing about science and science history. We would like to name a few of them; for those we have not space to name please accept our heartfelt thanks, including the many scientists we have interviewed. Their work has helped us better understand the overall nature of science.

We would like to express our heartfelt appreciation to James Warren, formerly of Facts On File, whose vision and enthusiastic encouragement helped shape the first edition; Frank K. Darmstadt, executive editor, whose boundless energy and support made all this book and its companions happen against impossible odds; and the rest of the Facts On File staff. A special thank you as well to Heather Lindsay of AIP Emilio Segrè Visual Archives, Lynne Farrington of the Annenberg Rare Book and Manuscript Library, Tracy Elizabeth Robinson and David Burgevin of the Smithsonian, and Shirley Neiman of Stock Montage, Inc. Our heartfelt gratitude also to Frances Spangenburg, even though she will never read this one, for her unflagging encouragement at every step of our writing careers.

And finally, our gratitude and affection to the late Morgan Sherwood and his wife, Jeanie Sherwood, for their warmth and generosity and their gift of Morgan's fine, extensive library on pseudoscience and the history of science.

INTRODUCTION

. . . the progress of science may be, I believe will be, step by step towards [a consummation], on many different roads converging towards it from all sides.

—William Thomson (Lord Kelvin), physicist

AS THE 19TH CENTURY DAWNED, a spirit of optimism and excitement buoyed much of the European continent as well as across the Atlantic, where the United States was very new—an experiment in reasonable, rational government. It was a time when women wore long skirts, men wore cravats, and the steam engine was just beginning to produce an effect on manufacturing methods and modes of travel. For science, it was an exciting time—sometimes referred to as the Golden Age of Science—a time when people flocked to lectures on scientific topics and humanity seemed on the verge of a better world, a world that would be made better through science.

This was the era that made an eccentric fictional private detective with a deerstalker cap into a hero, even though—probably because—he talked more like a logician than a rough-and-tumble private eye. Science had given society many gifts since the 16th century and at the beginning of the 19th century, the scene was quickly set for major breakthroughs, and it commanded attention. It was no longer an amateur's hobby, as it had been for Van Leeuwenhoek in the 17th century with the "wee beasties" he spied through his microscope and for William and Caroline Herschel in the 18th century as they gazed through their home-built telescope. Science had become a respected profession.

Two great breakthroughs would take place, both of which transformed the shape of people's lives. The first, the invention of the electric battery, graduated electricity from a static electricity parlor trick or party game into a force that ultimately would power billions of household lights and appliances, retail stores, and businesses the world over. The same battery opened the research doors to explore electromagnetic theory, the concept of the electromagnetic spectrum, and light on the theoretical side, as well as dynamos, generators, and electrolysis on the technological and experimental side. By the early 21st century, the simple battery cell created by a man named Alessandro Volta in 1800 has made possible a worldwide revolution in communication, information technology, and computing power that 19th-century citizens could scarcely have imagined.

The second revolutionary stroke came in the life sciences, where a theory known as "survival of the fittest" or evolution radically changed the way people thought about themselves, the Earth, the plants and animals around them, and the place of everything in the universe. No longer pictured as the pinnacle creation of a Supreme Being, humans came to a new level of self-knowledge and humility—and a greater sense than ever of their pure luck to have evolved so happily into thinking, sensing beings. This theory in particular, though solidly substantiated by evidence, has quite possibly stirred up more controversy than any other since Copernicus offered up his model of the solar system with the Sun, not Earth, at the center.

These are two of the big stories explored in this book, along with many others—stories about scientists and how they did science between the years of 1800 and 1895. But let's take a moment to explore the nature of science and how 19th-century men and women of science approached their work. In the 17th and 18th centuries, philosophers and thinkers tried to get away from the passive, "armchair" approach to figuring out what made the world tick that their ancient Greek predecessors had used. Instead, they began to use an approach that came to be known as the scientific method. Many argued that it was the only right way to arrive at sound solutions: First, to observe carefully and objectively. Second, to develop a hypothesis from which predictions can be made, which, in turn, can be tested. Third, to design and perform experiments that can offer irrefutable proof. (For more about the methods of science, see the preface.)

But by the beginning of the 19th century, scientists began to realize that most problems can be approached fruitfully from more than one direction. Some problems respond better to one type of attack, some to another. English theorists began using a model to represent—not necessarily the object itself—but how one might think of a structure or relationship. The model was not intended to represent literal reality. It just helped visualize the interaction of molecules in a chemical reaction, the steps of a physiological process, or the physical properties of a droplet of water sliding down a windowpane.

Intuition also paid off sometimes. Many scientists begin by working on a hunch. Or they may begin a particular line of reasoning for reasons as vague as it "seems right." Then they devise a series of objective tests to see if they were right.

By the end of the century, even mathematical proofs sometimes won the day, for lack of any more tangible experimental method for tackling a problem.

But the big thing to remember, regardless of approach, is that science is self-correcting. That is what makes science different from other human searches for truth. It can be a lot like working on a giant jigsaw puzzle. If, in the early stages of the puzzle, you put a piece in the wrong place, you eventually see where you have gone wrong as the rest of the picture emerges. You can spot where you have placed a piece of shrub in the middle of the sky, or attached a horse's tail to a pollywog. And you can change the mispositioned pieces around.

But the out-of-place puzzle piece can also be productive. Other pieces that fit with it may cluster around it and the whole assemblage may be moved to a new spot in the picture that makes it all work. And this is one of the fascinating aspects of the dynamic of science as it grows—one we have had to leave out of this book for the most part, unfortunately, for lack of space. One can easily get the impression in reading a history of science that everything moves surely forward, one discovery leading smoothly to another. In fact, science moves by fits and starts, with volumes of data collected that may seem contradictory or appear to lead nowhere. Many perfectly sensible-sounding theories get offered that are cast aside in favor of another—sometimes rightly, sometimes wrongly. The cast-offs are sometimes resurrected later. Or some pieces of a "wrong" theory may suddenly be seen to fit with a piece of another. It all contributes to the pot of knowledge and it is all part of the dynamics of an expanding understanding of the universe and how it works.

The 1800s arrived bringing a key fundamental discovery and a simple invention—a theory set forth by a teacher named Dalton in

England, and the battery invented by a physicist named Volta in Italy. Complemented by Darwin's theory in the life sciences, Dalton's discovery and Volta's battery set the stage for breakthroughs that continued throughout the century and affected not only how people viewed the universe but also the way they lived their daily lives.

PART I

The Physical Sciences in the Nineteenth Century

1

Atoms and Elements

Nothing exists except atoms and empty space; everything else is opinion.

—Democritus

John Dalton's dark, broad-brimmed hat and somber clothes silhouetted starkly against the gray skies of northern England as he took his daily hikes through the hillsides around Manchester. As the smoke from the growing industrial city's stacks mixed with the dank fog of the moors, Dalton took meticulous meteorological measurements, noted the continual changes of the Lancashire County weather, made studies of the atmosphere, and performed experiments. To his neighbors he seemed an odd and solitary figure. But to science this reclusive, scantily educated, individualistic Quaker became one of the great catalysts of the early 19th century, formulating one of the most basic theories of modern science, a theory that would become the foundation for modern chemistry and physics.

To John Dalton goes the credit for reestablishing the ancient idea of the atom, to which he first alluded at the end of a paper in 1803, and by 1826 his renown was widespread. In that year, at a meeting of the Royal Society, Britain's prestigious society of scientists, chemist-physicist Humphry Davy (whom we meet later in this chapter) proclaimed:

Mr. Dalton's permanent reputation will rest upon his having discovered a simple principle, universally applicable in the facts of

3

John Dalton developed a revision of atomic theory, first introduced by the ancient Greek philosopher Democritus. Dalton's fresh look at the idea of the atom opened up many new avenues for 19th-century scientists to travel. *(AIP Emilio Segrè Visual Archives)*

chemistry . . . and thus laying the foundation for future labours. . . . His merits in this respect resemble those of Kepler in astronomy.

John Dalton was not, however, the first to come up with the idea.

Nature's Building Blocks

Far back in time most ancient peoples had speculated that all substances were made of a few basic elements. The Greeks thought in terms of four fundamental substances that they called elements: air, fire, water, and earth. Hindus who subscribed to Ayurvedic philosophy imported the four-element theory from the Greeks, and ancient Chinese Taoists developed a theory of five interacting elemental "phases": metal, water, wood, fire, and earth.

But most of these ancient philosophies did not include the idea of atoms. Sometime in the fifth century B.C.E., a lone Greek thinker named Leucippus [lyoo-SIP-us] wondered what would happen if you broke a substance down to its smallest possible particle. What, for instance, if you split a rock in half, then split that in half, and again in half and again and again and again. Soon (sooner than you might suppose) you would have particles of dust. Could you split a bit of dust in half? Yes, speculated Leucippus (although, as far as we know, he did not try it). Then could you split it in half again? How far could you go? Eventually, Leucippus thought, you would reach the smallest possible particle, and this hypothetical mite, too small to be seen, he called an *atom*, the Greek word for "unsplittable."

His student Democritus (ca. 460 B.C.E.–ca. 370 B.C.E.) took up atomism as well and expanded on Leucippus's theory, maintaining that nothing but empty space existed between atoms and that all things, including the human mind, were composed of atoms, which moved mechanically, according to laws of nature. But familiar as these ideas sound today, Leucippus and Democritus arrived at their conclusions, not by experiment, but as the Greeks usually did, by considered reasoning. The Arab scientist Rhazes (ar-Razi, born ca. 865 C.E.) later held atomic views similar to those of Democritus and maintained that atoms gave rise to the four elements. By the 11th century scientists in India had developed a unique atomic theory, with combinations formed in dyads (combinations of two) and triads (combinations of three).

In the 17th century Robert Hooke (1635–1703) thought that the pressure exerted by a gas against the sides of a container (a balloon, for example) might be caused by a rush of atoms milling around. His contemporary Robert Boyle (1627–91) recognized early that gases were probably the key to understanding atoms (which he liked to call "corpuscles"). He showed, in a famous experiment with a

J-shaped tube, that air could be compressed. One good explanation for this, he thought, could be that the atoms in a gas were usually widely separated by empty space but moved closer together under pressure. It did not prove that atoms existed, though; a lot of other explanations were also possible.

Later, scientists in the 18th century discovered that water was composed of two elements, hydrogen and oxygen (so water was not an element after all). They also discovered what they referred to as different kinds of "air," gases that we now call oxygen, nitrogen, and carbon dioxide. Other elements had also been discovered by that time, too, and so the ancient ideas about how many elements there were and their identity no longer seemed valid. But the basic idea that all substances are composed of a relatively small number of elements still held.

The idea of the atom, though, did not generally catch on among most scientists at first. For one thing, two influential Greek thinkers, Plato (ca. 427 B.C.E.–347 B.C.E.) and Aristotle (384 B.C.E.–322 B.C.E.), did not subscribe to Leucippus and Democritus's idea, and though a few renegades existed, no one had ever shown compelling experimental evidence that pointed to the existence of atoms.

The "New Chemistry"

So the idea of the atom had been around a long time when John Dalton came on the scene, but no one had ever found a way to offer experimental proof that a tiny invisible building block of matter existed. They had also never found a way to explain the diverse chemical properties of the huge number of materials known even then.

Groundwork in chemistry had been laid in other ways, however. Antoine Lavoisier, Joseph Priestley, and Joseph Black had shown that chemistry, like physics, could profit enormously from the use of measurement. Primarily by weighing before and after, they began quantifying the results of their experiments and showed that sound theories and conclusions could be built on the basis of quantitative analysis.

Lavoisier also developed what has become known as the law of conservation of matter—the idea that matter is neither created nor destroyed but simply transformed. He also proposed that chemical elements are no more and no less than substances that one cannot break down into any simpler substance by chemical means. By the end of the 18th century, moreover, chemists had discovered a host of new elements not recognized before.

But it would be John Dalton's atomic theory that would provide an explanation of the structure operating behind the scenes.

Dalton's Atoms

As a young man John Dalton (1766–1844) hardly seemed destined to shake up the scientific world. He was never a great experimentalist. He was neither brilliant nor eloquent, and he had no access to the "best" schools. As a child he attended a one-room school, and at the age of 12 he took over teaching the entire school. In his spare time he read books by Newton and Boyle, and from that point on, for the most part, he was self-taught, unable to afford extended schooling.

Insight into Daltonism

John Dalton reached full adulthood before he realized that he did not see colors the way other people did. Pink looked blue to him, for example, and he could discern no trace of red in this delicate shade. At first he assumed that other people were confused. Only when he took an informal survey among a group of his friends and his brother did he discover that he and his brother were the only ones in the group to see blue when looking at pink, violet, and purple.

What caused this difference? Intrepid as always when it came to seeking answers, Dalton asked his assistant Joseph Ransome to dissect his eyeballs after his death—determined that science should solve this mystery (a disability that came to be called "daltonism"). Ransome investigated the fluids within the eye and the retina to look for clues but found nothing. So, preserved in a jar, Dalton's eyeballs came into the care of the Manchester Literary and Philosophical Society.

There a group of physiologists from Cambridge gained permission some 150 years later, in 1995, to test the DNA and genes for the three types of retinal cones that enable humans to see colors. Sure enough, they found a defect in the middle wavelength optical pigment—and Dalton's mystery was solved.

Soon afterward Dalton opened up his own school, but he was such a boring lecturer that within three years the school closed because all his students had dropped out.

Unlike many scientists of his day, Dalton never had much success on the lecture circuit. He had a gruff, country way about him, and his blunt manner completely lacked charisma. So, unable to pick up income as a lecturer, he supported himself most of his life as a teacher and tutor, pursuing his scientific interests in every remaining moment. (When asked why he never married, he replied dryly, "I haven't time. My head is too full of triangles, chemical processes, and electrical experiments to think of any such nonsense.")

A Friend, or Quaker, he strictly followed his religious custom of plain dress, which may have worked to his advantage, since he was color blind, and the choices of somber clothing in his closet included none in colors he could not see.

John Dalton had a great persistence about him, a methodical, consistent approach and an unflagging curiosity. He kept a daily meteorological diary his entire life from the year 1787 on, made several contributions to the study of gases, and gave the first clear statement of atomic theory—all part of his relentless delving into the mysteries of nature.

Many unsolved questions remained at the end of the 18th century about the nature of air and its components, and Dalton was fascinated. He made some 200,000 meteorological observations during his daily excursions over the course of his life—the last on the day of his death at age 78. Little wonder that his involvement in the study of the weather led him to explore the mysteries of gases, their behavior, and composition.

Air is composed mostly of oxygen, nitrogen, and water vapor, that much was already established—but why did the various parts of the mixture sometimes fail to separate out? Why didn't the heavier gas, nitrogen, sink to the bottom of a container or, for that matter, to the lower regions of the atmosphere? Using a simple, home-built apparatus, Dalton weighed the different elements of which air is composed and came to some important conclusions.

Dalton discovered that a mixture of gases weighed the same as the combined weight of the gases taken separately. As he explained it:

When two elastic fluids [gases] denoted by A and B are mixed together, there is no mutual repulsion between their particles; the particles of A do not repel those of B as they do one another. Consequently the pressure or whole weight upon any one particle arises solely from those of its own kind.

Known as Dalton's law of partial pressures (announced in 1801), basically the statement boils down to the idea that different gases in a mixture do not affect each other, or that the total pressure of a mixture of gases is the sum of the pressures of each gas taken singly. Dalton, of course, knew about Boyle's work with gases, and this new piece of information seemed to point even more strongly toward the idea that gases were made up of tiny, indivisible particles.

But he kept thinking about it. What if all matter—not just gases—was made up of these particles? Joseph Louis Proust had pointed out in 1788 that substances always combine in whole units. That is, chemicals might combine by a ratio of four to three. Or eight to one. But the reaction would not take, say, 8.673 grams of oxygen and 1.17 grams of hydrogen. One way to explain this law of definite proportions, as it was called, was to assume that each element was made of tiny particles, which, in honor of Democritus, he named "atoms." (This was a slightly confusing name, though Dalton could not know it, because as we now know, atoms are not really "unsplittable." They are, in turn, made up of several even tinier particles that appear to be unsplittable. For this reason many scientists today like to refer to Dalton's atom as the "chemical atom.") Dalton also pro-

⊙	Hydrogen	⊕	Soda	⊙⊕	Ammonia
⊕	Nitrogen	⊕	Pot Ash	⊙●	Olefiant
●	Carbon	○	Oxygen	○●	Carbonic Oxide
⊕	Sulphur	©	Copper	○●○	Carbonic Acid
⊘	Phosphorus	Ⓛ	Lead		Sulphuric Acid
⊙	Alumina	⊙○	Water		

Dalton's 1808 symbols and formulae

Dalton devised a new symbol for each element and listed the elements in ascending order by atomic weight, as closely as he could calculate it, based on the concept that the hydrogen atom had a value of 1.

Avogadro's Hypothesis

All gases, as Joseph Gay-Lussac showed definitely in 1802, expand to the same extent with a given increase in temperature. (John Dalton had also come to the same conclusion, and, independently, a man named Jacques Charles had anticipated both of them. This principle of the constant rate of expansion of gases at a constant pressure is now known as Charles's law, since Charles came up with it first.)

This law must mean, as a man named Amedeo Avogadro (1776–1856), count of Quaregna, announced in 1811, that equal volumes of different gases (at the same temperature) must contain the same number of particles (notice he did not say "atoms"). This idea, called Avogadro's hypothesis, stirred up considerable controversy throughout the first half of the 19th century.

If this were so, why did a given volume of oxygen or hydrogen weigh twice as much as one would expect from the atomic weight of these gases? (Oxygen and hydrogen atoms, we now know, occur in nature bound together in molecules of two—but in Avogadro's time this was not known.) If you chemically combine a volume of hydrogen and a volume of chlorine, Avogadro thought, you might expect to get one volume of hydrogen chloride gas. But instead you get two volumes. Did that mean that the hydrogen atoms and chlorine atoms were splitting to combine with each other? No, said Avogadro. Some elements, he hypothesized, might be combinations of atoms, and, in fact, he thought that some gases—including oxygen, nitrogen, and hydrogen—occurred naturally in molecules composed of two atoms (O_2, N_2, H_2). (Avogadro was the first to use the word *molecule,* which means "little mass," in this sense, and he was the first to distinguish in this way between atoms and molecules.) However, many major figures in chemistry—among them Dalton and the renowned Swedish chemist Jöns Jacob Berzelius—rejected the idea on the assumption that like atoms repel, and Avogadro's hypothesis remained dormant for many years, until 1858, when it finally became accepted.

posed that atoms of different chemical substances were not the same, as some earlier atomists had claimed. But, unlike Democritus, who thought that the atoms of different substances differed in shape, Dalton observed that they differed in weight, and he established the fact that each element has a weight of its own, particular to that element.

In September 1803 Dalton presented his first list of atomic weights based on hydrogen as a unit of one, with all other elements weighing multiples of that weight. He later expanded his original list to include 21 elements.

Thanks to Dalton, chemists began to realize that there were different types of atoms and that atoms of any one element were all alike, with specific properties and differing in relative weight from the atoms of all other elements.

Dalton kept pushing on the idea. Two elements, it seemed, might combine to form more than one compound. Carbon and oxygen, for example, combined to form what we now call carbon monoxide and also carbon dioxide. But they combine in different proportions, still always whole numbers (a ratio of 3:4 by weight in carbon dioxide). Dalton surmised that carbon monoxide might be just one particle of carbon combined with one of oxygen (with four carbon particles equal in weight to three of oxygen). Carbon dioxide, he figured, was one particle of carbon united with two of oxygen (a hypothesis that was later confirmed). Known as the law of multiple proportions, which Dalton published in 1804, a scientist named William Higgins in 1789 had anticipated this idea, but no one had supported it with experimental evidence until Dalton came along. Many of Dalton's colleagues found it exciting because it seemed to make the atomic theory even more plausible.

Dalton came up with this idea because he noticed that when elements combined chemically to form a compound, one or more atoms of one element combined with one or a small number of atoms from the other to form a molecule, the smallest particle of a compound. For instance a molecule of water is always composed of one part, by weight, of oxygen to two parts hydrogen. A molecule of water always has the same molecular weight as every other molecule of water, and it is the same as the weight of two atoms of hydrogen and one atom of oxygen. Dalton tested this out with several dozen compounds and always got the same results.

Dalton's theory of the atom made it possible to explain how these elements combined to form compound substances. Atoms got together, he said, to form other substances, and when they did, they combined chemically one with one, or one with two or three or so—always whole numbers, not split—to form other substances.

In 1808 he published his ideas in his *New System of Chemical Philosophy*. The atom, he declared, was the basic unit of the chemical element, and each chemical atom had its own particular weight. He wrote:

> There are three distinctions in the kinds of bodies, or three states, which have more specially claimed the attention of philosophical chemists; namely, those which are marked by the terms elastic fluids [gases], liquids, and solids. A very famous instance is exhibited to us in water, of a body, which, in certain circumstances, is capable of assuming all three states. In steam we recognize a perfectly elastic fluid, in water a perfect liquid, and in ice a complete solid. These observations have tacitly led to the conclusion which seems universally adopted, that all bodies of sensible magnitude, whether liquid or solid, are constituted of a vast number of extremely small particles, or atoms of matter bound together by a force of attraction, which is more or less powerful according to circumstances. . . .

He went on to explain that chemical analysis and synthesis simply involved reorganizing these particles—separating them from each other or joining them together. As Lavoisier had said, matter was neither created nor destroyed in the process. "All the changes we can produce," Dalton declared, "consist in separating particles that are in a state of cohesion or combination, and joining those that were previously at a distance." These are all insights that still hold firm today.

Dalton's atomic theory found success where others had failed because he provided a model from which definite predictions could be made. Some features of his theory, certainly, were later set aside, but the core features survived: that each atom has a characteristic mass and that atoms of the elements remain unchanged by chemical processes.

Along the way Dalton came up with some other, less major discoveries. He was the first to publish the generalization that when any gas starts out at the same temperature as another gas, both will expand equally when heated to the same higher temperature. He was also the first to describe color blindness, in a paper published in 1794.

In 1833 a group of admirers and friends collected contributions to build a statue of Dalton, which was erected in front of the Manchester Royal Institution. Several prestigious societies honored him, including the Royal Society in London and the Academy of Sciences in Paris. In 1832, when he received a doctorate from Oxford, he had the opportunity to be presented to the king of England. The only problem was he would be required to wear court dress, including a sword, which was directly contrary to the pacifist principles of his religion. But he and British dignitaries settled on a compromise; he would wear the cloak of Oxford, which would make the question of the sword a moot point. He may or may not have known that the cloak he wore was bright red—also completely out of keeping with Quaker custom. But to the color-blind scientist, the cloak was gray.

John Dalton died in 1844, much respected for his work on atomic theory and the behavior of gases. More than 40,000 people filed by the coffin of the man who couldn't seem to get students to come to his classes. He had set the stage early in his life for the greatest 19th-century developments in both physics and chemistry, and he was lucky enough to have seen the day when people recognized the value of his contribution.

The Electric Connection

The story will return to the saga of atoms and elements in chemistry, but first a side trip to Luigi Galvani's laboratory in Bologna, Italy. It is the summer of 1771, a few years before our 19th-century story begins. The laboratory is a mess, with dozens of pairs of frog legs (possibly destined for a pot of soup, according to some accounts) strewn across the wooden tabletop.

Luigi Galvani [gahl-VAH-nee] (1737–98) was an anatomist and a physician, not a physicist. He was professor of biology at the University of Bologna. But it came to Galvani's mind to try stimulating the muscles of the dissected frog legs with a spark from an electric machine. The frog legs twitched on contact.

Luigi Galvani studied how electricity affected animal nerves and muscles. *(Courtesy of the National Library of Medicine)*

If an electrical spark caused this muscle twitching, Galvani reasoned, then he could confirm, as American scientist Benjamin Franklin had postulated from his kite experiment, that lightning was indeed electricity. Galvani hung frog legs from brass hooks against an iron latticework to test his premise. When thunderstorms came by, the legs twitched. But something else happened: They also twitched when there were no thunderstorms. The twitching occurred, Galvani found, whenever the muscles came in contact with two different metals at the same time.

Galvani was not really sure what the cause of this phenomenon was. Did the metals cause the twitching? Or did the muscles, even though dead, retain a sort of innate "animal electricity"? Maybe Galvani's interests in biology led him to lean toward the idea that the animal tissue of the frog legs possessed the electrical force he saw. But he published his results in 1791 and sparked a kind of revolution when another Italian, Alessandro Volta, saw Galvani's publication and also began working on the problem.

Volta (1745–1827) read Galvani's *Commentaries*, repeated his experiments and tried another one on himself. He tried putting a piece of tinfoil and a silver coin in his mouth—one on top of his tongue, the other touching his tongue's lower surface, connecting them with a copper wire. He found that this rigging produced a distinctive sour taste in his mouth. He correctly surmised that this sour taste indicated the presence of an electrical charge.

"It is also worthy of note," he wrote, "that this taste lasts as long as the tin and silver are in contact with each other . . . this shows that the flow of electricity from one place to another, is continuing without interruption."

The metals, he realized, were not just conductors—they were actually producing the electricity themselves! Galvani was wrong; the frog legs had exhibited not animal electricity but metallic electricity. However, Galvani had played an important role, drawing attention by his experiment to a fact that would dramatically open the door to the study of electricity, its use as a valuable tool in science, and the countless industrial and commercial uses found for it in the 150 years since. His name has become a household word in expressions such as *galvanized by fear* and terms such as *galvanized iron* and *galvanometer*, an instrument designed to detect electric current.

In 1797 Volta had succeeded in producing current electricity—not the static form of electricity of the Leyden jar, which had been the best available up to that time. In 1800 he wrote to the Royal Society in London, describing the first battery, a continuous source of electric current.

Davy's Electrochemistry

Electricity held great fascination for everyone—in both scientific and social circles—at the end of the 18th century. Everyone was talking about Benjamin Franklin's experiments with a kite string and lightning, and socialites delighted in playing with static electricity at picnics and parties. But no one had succeeded in finding out much about what it was or how it worked, partly because no continuous source of it existed.

Not, that is, until Alessandro Volta invented what came to be known as the voltaic cell (see sidebar). Volta's work not only opened up avenues for exploring the nature of electricity (producing spectacular results, both in theoretical physics and industry) but also provided chemistry with a breakthrough tool for discovering new elements and exploring the nature of chemical bonding.

And here our story doubles back to chemistry. No sooner had Volta communicated his findings to the Royal Society in London than another young scientist, Humphry Davy, began thinking about a way the voltaic cell could be used to solve some problems in chemistry. Davy, who is probably best known for his discovery of two elements, sodium and potassium, and for his invention of a safety lamp for miners, was hired in 1800 (along with Thomas Young, whose work we discuss in chapter Four) to join the staff of the Royal Institution, a newly founded research laboratory and educational institution.

Davy was the oldest of five children, born in 1778, the son of a woodcarver in the town of Penzance on the western coast of Cornwall, England. In 1794, when young Davy was only 16, his father died, leaving the boy to support his family. So Humphry shortly began an apprenticeship with a local surgeon, but by the time he was 19, he developed a keen interest in experimental chemistry and the boundary between chemistry and physics. He began to test the ideas in Antoine Lavoisier's *Traité élémentaire de chimie* (1789) and came to some revolutionary conclusions for the time. Based on observations he made while rubbing blocks of ice together, he asserted that heat was not an "imponderable fluid," as most chemists of the time thought, but a form of motion. Unfortunately

Volta and the Birth of the Battery

Alessandro Volta began the age of electricity in 1800 when he announced his invention of the electric battery, the first continuous source of electric current. Not that studies of electricity had not been made before; scientists worldwide (including Benjamin Franklin) had made studies of static electricity for a century. But static electricity discharged all at one time, in a single spark or jolt. Volta's battery could provide a current, and while practical uses were not found for it for several years, chemists and physicists immediately set it to work as a tool in analyzing substances.

Volta, a physicist at the University of Pisa, got his first inspiration from the work of Galvani on frogs (see text), and did some experiments of his own. Skeptical about "animal electricity," he was struck by the fact that electricity was produced only if two different metals were used. Also, he noticed, some combinations of metals produced more twitching than others. When he placed tinfoil and silver on his tongue, which is mostly muscle, his tongue did not twitch much, but he did notice a sour taste. This made him wonder if the electricity might be conducted from one metal to the other by the fluid of his saliva. Volta experimented with many solutions, finally settling on brine, which is a strong saltwater solution. He found that if he constructed piles of dissimilar metal disks, sandwiching pieces of cardboard soaked in brine between them, he had a very effective set of battery cells (each sandwich forming one cell). The resultant stack became known as the voltaic cell, named after its inventor.

Its potential was immediately recognized by scientists everywhere, even by Napoleon in France, who had made Volta a count and a senator in the scientist's native Lombardy (which had recently been conquered by Napoleon). In a letter to the Royal Society in London in 1800, Volta expressed his own delight in his invention's wonderful simplicity. "Yes!" he wrote in his letter, "the apparatus of which I speak, and which doubtless will astonish you, is only an assemblage of a number of good conductors of different sorts arranged in a certain way."

Alessandro Volta's astonishing "assemblage," often referred to as a "voltaic pile," became a tool as important to science as the telescope and the microscope long before it came to transform the way people lit their homes and streets.

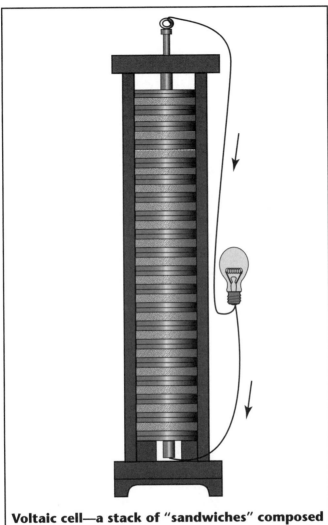

Voltaic cell—a stack of "sandwiches" composed of brine-soaked cardboard disks between disks made of two different types of metal

Alessandro Volta's battery, known as the "voltaic cell," offered the first source of continuous electric current. Because of its far-reaching effect on people's lives, this invention is arguably the most significant and wide-reaching breakthrough of the 19th century.

Davy was young and a little reckless, and he spoke with more confidence than his experiments warranted. As a result the scientific community greeted his announcement rather coolly, with a large dose of skepticism, and Davy was deeply disappointed.

But in 1798 Davy became an assistant to Thomas Beddoes, a versatile chemist and physician specializing in the therapeutic uses of gases. At Beddoes's Pneumatic Institution in Bristol, Davy experimented, using himself as a guinea pig. He discovered how to prepare nitrous oxide (sometimes called laughing gas, which became used widely by dentists), of which he breathed some 16 quarts all in one day, an experience he later said "completely intoxicated" him. He investigated the physiological effects of the gas and wrote a well-reasoned paper on it in 1799, which succeeded in establishing his reputation as a chemist (and attained notoriety among several figures in society, including the poets Coleridge and Wordsworth, who enjoyed visiting his lab to experiment with the intoxicating effects of his discovery).

Davy's scientific paper on nitrous oxide caught the eye of Count Rumford, a colorful American-born figure, whose work on heat as motion also had stirred up considerable controversy in the preceding decade at a time when most chemists and physicists thought heat was caused by an imponderable fluid (that is, a fluid having no weight) called "caloric." Though working at the time for the government of Bavaria, Rumford, originally known as Benjamin Thompson, had come up with the idea of founding a Royal Institution in Britain to popularize science and apply its discoveries to everyday life, the arts, and manufacturing. Rumford hired Davy as the first director of the laboratory, a great break for the aspiring young chemist.

The year was 1800. Before he left Bristol for London, Davy had established to his own satisfaction that Volta's cell was producing electricity through chemical reaction, and he was quick to surmise that the reverse might also be true: that the use of electricity on compounds and mixtures might in turn produce chemical reactions.

However, over the next few years, his duties in London at the Royal Institution took him away from the subject. To raise money, the institution developed a highly popular lecture series, and Davy's charisma and enthusiasm took him far as one of the best lecturers of his day. (His spectacular demonstrations with electricity and amusing exhibitions of the "highs" produced by nitrous oxide probably added to his popularity.) Probably as much to keep a firm financial footing as to pursue the ideals of popularization, the institution focused on agricultural science, tanning, and mineralogy, and Davy's several excellent papers on these subjects not only added to the stature of the institution but also enhanced his own.

But in 1806 he saw his opportunity. In the space of five weeks, he performed 108 experiments in electrolysis, the use of electricity to produce chemical changes. In one brilliant coup that year, in a lec-

Humphry Davy, recognized as the founder of electrochemistry, was also handsome, debonair, and charming. *(AIP Emilio Segrè Visual Archives)*

ture "On Some Chemical Agencies of Electricity" to the prestigious Royal Society, Davy established theoretical links between electrolysis and voltaic action, and he gave one of the first explanations—certainly the first important one—of the electrical nature of chemical reaction. Substances combine chemically, he said, because of a mutual electrical attraction between atoms.

Davy also thought that electricity might be used to break the bonds between parts of compounds to isolate elements not yet discovered. Scientists had been working on several substances for years—lime, magnesia, potash, and others—that seemed to be oxides of metals. But no amount of heat, or any other method anyone could think of, had ever succeeded in breaking the tightly held oxygen away. At the end of his presentation in 1806, he prophetically mentioned his hope "that the new mode of analysis may lead us to the discovery of the *true* elements of bodies."

To try this trick, Davy built a huge battery, composed of more than 250 metal plates and much more powerful than Volta's little piles of metal disks and cardboard. The following year, working with a lump of very slightly dampened potash (a substance formed by soaking the ashes of burnt plants in pots of water), he attached an insulated metal electrode from the negative side of a battery to one surface of the lump. To another surface of the potash lump, he attached a metal wire running to the positive side of the battery, which, he noted, "was in an intense state of activity." At both points of contact, the potash began to fuse, giving off a gas on the surface that was attached to the positive pole. At the other contact point, no gas was given off, but "small globules having a high metallic lustre" began to form. They looked a lot like droplets of mercury and some of them burned brightly and exploded. Davy knew immediately that he had discovered a new element, which he called potassium (after "potash"). As his brother, John, wrote describing the experiment, when Humphry Davy "saw the minute globules of potassium burst through the crust of potash, and take fire as they entered the atmosphere, he could not contain his joy—he actually bounded about the room in ecstatic delight; and some little time was required for him to compose himself sufficiently to continue the experiment."

A few days later Davy used the same process on soda (now known as sodium hydroxide) and discovered sodium. The trick was working. Meanwhile, in Stockholm, Jöns Jacob Berzelius and his colleagues were pursuing similar experiments, and communications flew back and forth. Berzelius had found that he got an "amalgam," or alloy of some other metal with mercury, when he ran a current through a mercury compound added to lime or baryta. That gave Davy another key, and within a few months, by applying a strong heat to the amalgams Berzelius described (and to others), he also isolated magnesium (from magnesia), calcium (named after "calx"), strontium (from a mineral named for a Scottish town called Strontian), and barium (from baryta). Davy was racking up an impressive list of discoveries. To Davy also goes the credit for testing a green gas called oxymuriatic acid and recognizing it in 1810 as an element that he called chlorine (for its greenish color).

The year 1812 was a watershed for Davy, the year in which he published his *Elements of Chemical Philosophy*. He followed up quickly with the more applied *Elements of Agricultural Chemistry*. He was knighted, in recognition of his accomplishments, in April 1812 and shortly thereafter married Jane Apreece, a wealthy Scottish widow. In 1813 he resigned his position as professor at the Royal Institution and set off for Europe with his new wife and a young assistant he had recently taken on, Michael Faraday, whose story figures large later in the century. Despite the fact that England was at war with France at the time, as Davy remarked, "There is never a war among men of science," and Napoleon welcomed Davy's visit, during which Davy and Faraday called on many of the prominent scientists on the Continent. For Faraday the trip was a stunning introduction to the cutting edge of science.

Davy became president of the Royal Society in 1820 and began working on a means to prevent corrosion of the copper sheathings on ship bottoms, but he became ill and spent most of his time after 1823 in Switzerland, where he died at the age of 51. There his stature was so great that he was given a state funeral.

The year was 1829, and for chemistry the century had only just begun, bolstered by the atomic theory of John Dalton, the new tool invented by Volta, and the extraordinary discoveries of new elements made by Davy and others. New challenges lay ahead: to find order in the chaos of new elements, to continue to search out more new elements, and to make sense of the vast jungle of molecules that form with the element carbon. Progress in all these fields was soon to come.

2
Chemistry's Perplexing World of Complexity and Order

BY 1830 THE NUMBER OF known elements had swelled to 54. In addition to the six discovered by Davy between 1807 and 1808, 10 more had turned up, including boron, iodine, lithium, silicon, bromine, and aluminum. Obviously more than "a few simple elements" made up the stuff of the universe, and instead of the convergence the century had seemed to promise, confusion now seemed to reign in chemistry.

For one thing no one used the same symbols to mean the same thing. Many strange, mysterious signs still persisted, borrowed long ago by the alchemists from astrology. For gold the symbol was a circle with a dot in the center; for silver a crescent. The symbol for sulfur was a triangle pointing upward, and for antimony a little crown. Most of these made no real sense to anyone. Dalton had offered a system that used a circle differentiated in some way for every element. But even this was difficult to remember. Finally, in 1826, Berzelius came up with the simple idea of using the first letter of each element's name as its symbol. O was oxygen, N was nitrogen, S was sulfur, and so on. When an initial letter was already taken, the next distinguishing letter was added. So calcium was Ca and chlorine was Cl. This system is still in use today. Some confusion still existed between languages: German chemists called one element Stickstoff, while the French called it azote, and the English called it nitrogen. So Berzelius settled on the latinized names as his sources, and the symbols were adopted internationally. Luckily for those

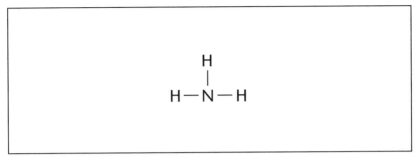

The structure of an ammonia molecule

whose language is English, most elements were already known by their latinized names, with a few exceptions such as gold (Au from aurum), silver (Ag from argentum), and sodium (Na from natrium).

Friedrich Kekulé von Stradonitz [KAY-koo-lay] also came up with an idea for arranging atomic symbols in structured diagrams, representing the arrangement of atoms in molecules. In Kekulé's system, water (H_2O), for example, became H—O—H. Likewise the three hydrogen atoms of ammonia (NH_3) clustered in a triangle around the lone nitrogen atom. Soon Kekulé's structures caught on.

But controversy reigned about the formulas for even the most common compounds. No one could agree about the atomic weights of the various elements, and many confused atoms with molecules in writing formulas. For even such a common compound as acetic acid (vinegar), various factions of chemists touted as many as 19 different formulas.

The Karlsruhe Conference

Something had to be done. At the heart of the movement stood Kekulé, who called the first international scientific conference to try to clean up the mess in chemistry. The First International Chemical Conference, as it was called, took place in 1860 in the small town of Karlsruhe, Germany, on the banks of the Rhine River, just across the border from France. A total of 140 delegates attended, including most of the prominent chemists of the day.

But this was a group of adamant and opinionated scientists, and the conference got off to a stormy start, with little agreement on anything, certainly not on atomic weights. Then Stanislao Cannizzaro took the floor.

Cannizzaro was a fiery, combative individual who was accustomed to conflict. In fact he had fled to France in 1848 from his native Sicily to avoid punishment for fighting on the losing side of a Sicilian insurrection against the then-ruling government of Naples. In France he had been giving considerable thought to the mess chemistry was in. In 1858 he had published a paper resurrecting Avogadro's hypothesis, which no one had thought about for almost 50 years—the idea that equal volumes of different gases (at the same temperature) must contain the same number of particles. He arrived in Karlsruhe prepared with a fiery defense of atomic weight, Avogadro's hypothesis, and a clear distinction between atoms and molecules. Use Avogadro's hypothesis to determine the molecular weight of gases, he said. Use Gay-Lussac's law of combining volumes. And use Berzelius's atomic weights. With this combination Cannizzaro maintained that many of the problems would be resolved. He backed up his speech with pamphlets, convincing some at the conference and many more shortly thereafter. One, in particular, would go back to Russia and think about it a great deal.

Mendeleyev's Solitaire

With his long hair flying in the wind, graying beard, and commanding posture, Dmitry Mendeleyev [men-deh-LAY-ef] looked more like a biblical prophet than a patriarch of the sciences the day he single-handedly piloted his tiny basket high into the skies beneath a giant balloon. The year was 1887, and he wanted to photograph a solar eclipse from the closest, best vantage point he could get. That meant a balloon, a one-person craft. So, not to be stopped at the brink of such an opportunity, Mendeleyev took off, took his photographs, and landed, even though he did not know the first thing about flying such a contraption. He was a flamboyant individual of principle and courage, unafraid of skeptics, naysayers, political pressures, or airborne craft. A native of Siberia he was the magician who some 18 years earlier had brought order to the chaotic mess of elements chemists had by that time discovered. He was also the first scientist from the Russian empire whose work made a timely impact in Europe, and in 1955, nearly 50 years after his death, his extraordinary contributions to chemistry and physics received the perfect tribute: a newly discovered element, mendelevium, named in his honor.

Possibly of Mongolian descent on his mother's side, Mendeleyev (1834–1907) was the youngest of a very large family of some 16 or 17 children, grandson of the first newspaper publisher in Siberia; his father was the local high school principal and his resourceful mother ran a glass factory. Mendeleyev learned science as a child from a political prisoner who had been banished to Siberia as punishment. But Mendeleyev's father died while he was in his early teens and his mother's glass factory burned down soon after her husband's death. So, with most of her children grown, his mother set out in 1849 for the big cities of Russia to gain admittance to college for her youngest. She succeeded in St. Petersburg, where Mendeleyev was admitted to the university with the help of a friend of his father.

After graduating in 1855, Mendeleyev set out for France and Germany in 1859 for graduate studies in chemistry. While there, he worked with Robert Wilhelm Bunsen (who invented the Bunsen burner) and attended the First International Chemical Conference at Karlsruhe. The strong arguments Cannizzaro had made there concerning atomic weights continued to intrigue Mendeleyev when he returned to St. Petersburg, where he began teaching at the university in 1861 and received an appointment as professor of technical chemistry in 1866.

Some scientists had speculated that closeness in atomic weight might be related to similarities among the elements. Cobalt and nickel, for example, had atomic weights so close that most chemists at the time could not differentiate them, and their characteristics were very similar. But the hypothesis did not hold up. Take chlorine and sulfur, with atomic weights of approximately 35.5 and 32, respectively. One is a

The eccentric Russian scientist Dmitry Mendeleyev developed the concept known as the "periodic table," which helped chemists recognize the systematic relationships among the elements. *(AIP Emilio Segrè Visual Archives, W. F. Meggers Collection)*

yellowish-green gas, the other a yellow solid—strikingly different. So they began to look for other relationships. By 1861 a number of chemists had been playing around for several years with the idea of triads or small groups of elements that seemed to be "families," based on similarities in their properties. As early as 1817 Johann Wolfgang Döbereiner had begun to notice some consistent relationships in the atomic weights of certain groups of similar elements—with the middle member's atomic weight equal to the mean of the other two atomic weights. For example, in the triad of calcium, strontium, and barium, the atomic weight of strontium (figured at the time as 88) was roughly the mean of calcium's (40) and barium's (137). Likewise, the melting point of strontium (800 degrees C) lay between that of calcium (851 degrees C) and barium (710 degrees C). And calcium is considered active in chemical reactions, with barium more so and strontium—in between! The list of ways that strontium was "in between" calcium and barium went on and on. Such triad relationships were intriguing, and other scientists added to the idea.

In 1864 the London industrial chemist John Alexander Reina Newlands (1837–98) was the first to notice that a table of elements arranged by order of atomic weights showed a pattern in which "the eighth element, starting from a given one, is a kind of repetition of the first, like the eighth note in an octave of music." He called this discovery the "law of octaves," but he was virtually laughed out of the meeting of chemists at which he announced his ideas. Why not just alphabetize the elements to see what patterns you get? jibed George Carey Foster, a professor of physics. Newlands's table of elements did have some flaws, but he had in fact recognized a useful pattern. George Carey Foster, though a competent physicist, is known primarily for his taunting remark—illustrating that a scientific idea that may seem to go nowhere today can lead to new insights tomorrow, and ill-considered scoffing can come back to haunt the scoffer. More than 20 years later, the Royal Society awarded Newlands the Davy medal for his work, which also included organizing the elements in order of ascending atomic weight and assigning a number to each according to its position in his table.

But Dmitry Mendeleyev was the one who played with the idea of order among the elements the most creatively and pushed it to its most logical conclusions. Mendeleyev was fond of a type of solitaire game called patience. So he played patience with all the known elements, their symbols, atomic weights, and unique properties marked on cards. Then he started arranging them in groups. And he found that, if you lined the elements up in the order of increasing atomic weight, similar characteristics would occur every so often—periodically spaced. For example, he found that hydrogen (with an atomic weight of 1 and first on his list), fluorine (ninth on his list), and chlorine (in the seventeenth position) were spaced eight spaces apart, like Newlands's "octaves" and shared similar properties. He tried listing all the groups with similar properties in the same vertical column. And he began to work out a table, with atomic weight increasing from upper left to lower right, and families of elements stacked in columns.

But Mendeleyev's great daring was that, where elements would not fit into his scheme for the table, he played the game as he would a game of solitaire, recognizing that he might not have all the cards in his hand—some cards might still be in the deck. So, if a slot called for an element with certain properties, and there was no such element as far as anyone knew, then he left gaps in his table for the elements still in the deck—those not yet discovered. What is more, he even named some of them: eka-boron, eka-aluminum, and eka-silicon. Eka-aluminum was the gap in the column below aluminum, eka-silicon was the one below silicon. And he predicted their properties. His work, published in 1869, was translated immediately from Russian into German (in this he was far luckier than any Russian scientist before him, since Russian work was usually lost to the rest of the world for years because it went untranslated). But in Europe, everyone thought he was crazy, possibly even wrote him off as a Russian mystic.

Thumbprinting the Elements

As Mendeleyev was working on his periodic table, a wonderful new tool came on the scene: the spectroscope. It would prove highly useful not only for chemists but also for astronomers and physicists— and remains so today.

The idea began early in the century with the work of a young optician named Joseph von Fraunhofer. The son of a glazier, he was orphaned at 11 and became the apprentice of an optician. One baleful day the entire building he lived in collapsed around him, and he was the sole occupant to survive. But he was in luck. The elector of

Bavaria, Maximilian I, heard the tragic story and gave him enough money to start his own career as an optician.

Fraunhofer developed an international reputation for high quality and precision in his work, and several prominent astronomers used his prisms and optical instruments. In 1814, as he tested some lenses he was making, he made use of a prism, which, as Newton had shown a century earlier, could break the Sun's white light into the colors of the spectrum. As he did so he noticed some strange black lines that seemed to punctuate the solar spectrum—in fact he saw at least 600, some wider, some narrower, dividing portions of the spectrum. (Newton, using considerably less accurately ground prisms, probably could not see them because the imperfections of the glass would have made them fuzzy.)

Each color of the spectrum, Fraunhofer knew, correlates with a unique wavelength of light. (Light waves have crests and troughs, much like the waves of the ocean, and the measurement from one crest to the next is called a wavelength.) Shorter wavelengths fell at the violet end of the spectrum, while longer ones fell at the red end. Fraunhofer noticed that the position of the prominent lines in the spectrum always remained the same. The strange black lines seemed to be a kind of code. They definitely had some significance. He tried using different light sources—the direct light of the Sun and the reflected light of the Moon and planets. Then even starlight. Each different star, he found, seemed to leave a different code, a different thumbprint. But no one could crack the code, and Fraunhofer died in 1826 of tuberculosis at the age of 39 without ever finding out the meaning of the "Fraunhofer lines" named after him.

Half a century later a team of physicists at the University of Heidelberg—Gustav Kirchhoff and Robert Wilhelm Bunsen—developed an instrument they called a spectroscope, which passed light through a narrow slit before passing it through a prism. The slit controlled the source of the light, and, as a result, different wavelengths were displayed differently and, when viewed against a scale, became much easier to differentiate and interpret.

Using the special burner devised by Bunsen, which gave off very little light itself, Kirchhoff and Bunsen heated various chemicals to incandescence (the heat at which they gave off light) and noticed that each chemical gave off its own distinctive pattern of colored lines. Sodium vapor, for example, when brought to a glowing heat, produced a double yellow line: its thumbprint. Once the thumbprints of all the elements were known, any ore or compound—any substance, in fact—could be heated and its components could be analyzed in this way. What is more, the spectroscope could fingerprint extraordinarily tiny amounts of an element.

Kirchhoff and Bunsen first announced their invention publicly on October 27, 1859, and the spectroscope, inevitably, began to uncover new elements, one after another. Cesium, named after its distinctive blue spectral line, was discovered on May 10, 1860. Rubidium, named after the red line that tipped off its existence, was discovered the following year. A new run of elements had begun to flow.

Then in 1875 a French chemist named Paul Emile Lecoq de Boisbaudran [luh-KOHK-duh-bwah-boh-DRAHN] found a spectral line he had never seen before, in a hunk of zinc ore from the Pyrenees mountains. One of the first to enter the exciting new field in 1859, after searching with his spectroscope for 16 years he at last had found a new element. He called it gallium, after the Latin name for France (or, maybe, after himself, since *le coq* means "rooster" in French, which is *gallus* in Latin). When Mendeleyev read the description of the new element, he was elated. Gallium had almost exactly the same properties he had predicted for eka-aluminum! The new element slipped easily into its place on the periodic table, and suddenly everyone began to take Mendeleyev more seriously. The powerful tool of spectroscopy had won the day.

Another element, scandium (named for Scandinavia), discovered in 1879, fit almost perfectly in the place Mendeleyev had left for eka-boron. And in 1886, when the element germanium (named for Germany) was discovered, it filled the eka-silicon spot. For most people Mendeleyev's periodic law had finally gained acceptance. He had recognized a natural order, in the manner of every good scientist, where chaos had seemed to reign.

But no one knew why this order, this periodicity, existed. That required knowing abut the nucleus of the atom and its structure, and in the 19th century scientists were not yet ready to part with the idea that the atoms with which they were working were unsplittable. Yet, the way the number of elements kept steadily increasing, chemists seemed to be getting further and further away from the few simple building blocks of nature they had set out to find. The number would soon climb to over 90. (And the 20th and 21st centuries would see that number increase even further, with the many new elements created by nuclear chemists, up to number 116, ununhexium, as of 2001, and still counting.)

In the last five years of the century, John William Strutt, better known as the famous English physicist Lord Rayleigh, and his assistant, a Scottish chemist named William (later Sir William) Ramsay, repeated an experiment performed a hundred years earlier by Henry Cavendish, this time using the spectroscope. As a result, they discovered argon, and Ramsay went on in the following years to discover helium and, with Morris Travers, the inert (completely unreactive) gases neon, krypton, and xenon. For these, no slot remained in Mendeleyev's table. Could this be its downfall? But no, the answer was simple: The great Siberian card player was not clairvoyant; he had left out one entire column on the right-hand side of his table, which is where those elements reside today.

Birth of Organic Chemistry

Meanwhile, as Dalton, Davy, and Mendeleyev succeeded in revolutionizing inorganic chemistry, another, even more confusing, field was also undergoing a major transformation. In 1807 Berzelius named the class of chemicals that originated in living things organic and gave the name inorganic to those that did not. Organic substances, he maintained, functioned by completely different laws from their inorganic cousins and appeared in many ways to be vastly different. Most scientists, including Berzelius, assumed this difference came from the presence of some "vital" force that linked organic chemicals to the living or once-living matter in which they were found or by which they were produced. And no one had ever created an organic compound from inorganic substances. And, according to Berzelius, no one ever would.

Then one day in 1828, Friedrich Wöhler [VOH-ler], a student of Berzelius, was working in his laboratory on some problem having to do with cyanides, when he heated a quantity of ammonium cyanate. He was stunned to see the results: He had produced a compound that looked exactly like urea. This seemed highly unlikely, since urea, a component of urine, is the primary nitrogenous waste of mammals, unquestionably organic. Skeptical, Wöhler tested the substance he had produced. It was definitely urea. And on February 22, 1828, he announced to Berzelius that he had produced an organic compound out of an inorganic compound.

Berzelius, never easy to convince, made a case for the idea that ammonium cyanate can be seen as organic, not inorganic. So Wohler's discovery may have been a bit unsure—but other chemists were challenged by his achievement to try other inorganic compounds and found that, in fact, organic compounds can be synthesized from inorganic materials. Then in 1845 Adolph Wilhelm Hermann Kolbe succeeded for the first time in synthesizing an organic compound (acetic acid) directly from chemical elements. Perhaps no such thing as a "vital" force existed after all.

But, if not, then why did Jean-Baptiste Biot discover in 1815 that when he produced tartaric acid in the laboratory, it failed to polarize light (where the transverse vibrations of the light waves are confined to just one direction), when tartaric acid produced by grapes did polarize light? The two batches of acid had the same components in the same ratio, the same chemical formula. Justus von Liebig and Wohler found more such pairs in the 1820s. And in 1830 Berzelius, the great namer, gave the name *isomer* to pairs of compounds that had the same chemical formulas but behaved differently. "Organic chemistry," wrote Wohler in perplexity to Berzelius in 1835, "appears to me like a primeval forest of the tropics, full of the most remarkable things."

Louis Pasteur [pas-TUHR], whom we meet again later in this book, did his first serious work in chemistry on the strange problem that Biot had found with the tartaric acid isomers. Pasteur tried isolating single crystals of the laboratory-produced isomer and found that they in fact did polarize light. Some polarized in one direction and others in the opposite direction. By 1848 he had an answer. The two types of crystals canceled each other out in the substance made in the laboratory, which is why it appeared that the whole substance did not polarize light.

Kekulé's structural formulas, meanwhile, helped explain what was going on in some of these complex organic compounds, some of which bonded with double and triple bonds, which Kekulé's system could show with double and triple dashes. Isomers could have the same atoms in the same ratio but arranged differently. For example, ethyl alcohol can be represented as in the figure at the top of page 34.

And dimethyl ether, which has the same number of hydrogen, carbon, and oxygen atoms, can be shown like this as in the figure at the bottom of page 34.

Carbon atoms, Kekulé pointed out in 1858, could combine directly with each other (unlike most other atoms), forming lengthy and com-

Explosives, Dyes, Perfumes, and Plastics: Organic Gifts to Industry

From the unlikely raw materials of coal, water, and air, several lucrative chemical industries emerged in the 19th century: explosives, dyes, perfumes, and plastics.

The first synthetic explosive, nitrocellulose, was discovered completely by accident by Christian Schönbein in 1846. He had been working one day in his lab and used his wife's apron to wipe up some spilled chemicals—probably sulfuric and nitric acids. The apron—whose cellulose fibers combined dramatically with the acids—suddenly exploded and disappeared. Also known as guncotton, nitrocellulose caused many deaths by premature explosions in the early years of its use.

A cousin of nitrocellulose known as nitroglycerine was also discovered in 1846. Highly volatile and unstable it was used in tunneling and blasting, also sometimes with disastrous results. Ways were found to tame both substances so they could be used more safely, and the results are cordite and dynamite, respectively. The use of such modern explosives has transformed the construction of big engineering projects such as highways, bridges, tunnels, and dams, as well as mining.

An English chemist named William Perkin a decade later, in 1856, with the discovery of a dye made from aniline that produced the color mauve accidentally began another chemical industry. Actually he was trying to make synthetic quinine (used to treat malaria), but mauve dye soon made him wealthy. Aniline, Perkin found, was not available on the open market, so he manufactured it from benzene, whose structure Kekulé would

plex chains. Since carbon atoms have a valency of four, he explained, they always combine with exactly four other atoms. Also he made clear that, by studying the products of a reaction, one could draw conclusions about the molecular structure of an organic molecule.

In 1861 Kekulé published the first volume of his textbook on organic chemistry. In it he cut through a long-term, entangled controversy with a simple, clean stroke. He defined organic molecules simply as those that contained carbon and inorganic molecules as those that did not. He made no reference to the issue of living or once-living substance. It was a blow against the idea that organic molecules

soon unlock. His colleague and teacher, German chemist August Wilhelm von Hofmann, discovered how to make a magenta dye the following year, and Germany soon became the seat of a very profitable chemical-dye industry. An orange-red crystalline named alizarin was synthesized in German by Karl Graebe in 1868, followed by indigo, synthesized by Adolf von Baeyer in 1880. (In a sort of side benefit to science, biologists soon found that certain plant and, especially, animal cells were easier to see under a microscope when stained with some of these dyes.) Graebe contributed to structural understanding of organic molecules by extending Kekulé's benzene ring to the structure of naphthalene, and Baeyer formulated the structure of indigo in 1883.

In 1868 Perkin scored again by producing the first synthesized perfume ingredient, coumarin, and from this discovery another great industry grew.

Meanwhile plastics got their start in the 19th century as well, with the synthesis of celluloid. The English chemist Alexander Parkes first converted the explosive nitrocellulose to a useful nonexplosive (though flammable) substance in 1855. Soon afterward the American inventor John Wesley Hyatt was looking for a better billiard ball in an age when they were made of ivory, and he improved on Parkes's celluloid for the purpose. English and American chemists dominate the plastics field to this day, and a wide array of types have been invented in the 20th and 21st centuries. The varieties seem endless, ranging from textiles such as rayon, nylon, and polyester to moldable, solid plastics—sometimes pliable, sometimes rigid—used for everything from plumbing pipes to toothbrushes, and from drinking straws to shower curtains.

somehow contained an indefinable "vital force," and it offered a new and useful way of looking at the field of organic chemistry.

Grabbing the Ring

For organic chemistry another problem still remained. No one had yet been able to explain the structure of benzene (C_6H_6), a coal tar product discovered by Michael Faraday in 1825. Of course, even without knowing the structure of benzene, William Perkin (see sidebar) and others working in the synthesis of dyes had been making progress. But

$$H-\underset{\underset{\displaystyle H}{|}}{\overset{\overset{\displaystyle H}{|}}{C}}-\underset{\underset{\displaystyle H}{|}}{\overset{\overset{\displaystyle H}{|}}{C}}-O-H$$

The structure of ethyl alcohol

no one could show how these atoms could fit together with each other in a way that explained how this molecule typically combined.

Then, one day in 1865, as Kekulé later wrote:

> I was sitting, writing at my text-book; but the work did not progress; my thoughts were elsewhere. I turned my chair to the fire and dozed. Again the atoms were gambolling before my eyes. This time the smaller groups kept mostly in the background. My mental eye, rendered more acute by repeated visions of this kind, could now distinguish larger structures, of manifold conformation: long rows, sometimes more closely fitting together; all twining and twisting in snake-like motion. But look! What was that? One of the snakes had

$$H-\underset{\underset{\displaystyle H}{|}}{\overset{\overset{\displaystyle H}{|}}{C}}-O-\underset{\underset{\displaystyle H}{|}}{\overset{\overset{\displaystyle H}{|}}{C}}-H$$

The structure of dimethyl ether

seized hold of its own tail, and the form whirled mockingly before my eyes. As if by a flash of lightning I awoke; and this time also I spent the rest of the night working out the consequence of the hypothesis.

What Kekulé came up with was what we now call the benzene ring, a molecule composed of benzene's carbon and hydrogen molecules arranged not in an open chain but in a closed hexagon, with alternate single and double bonds in rapid oscillation. (See figure on page 36.)

A Dutch chemist, Jacobus Van't Hoff, translated many of Kekulé's structural ideas into three-dimensional models that served to clarify much of organic chemistry, including the isomer puzzle that Biot and Pasteur had worked on. Kekulé's structural insights brought order to organic chemistry where at the beginning of the century incredible confusion had existed, and though many theoretical refinements have been made since, his ideas still serve to guide chemists through the thicket of synthesis and provide a model that visualizes the organic molecule and predicts its reactions.

For chemistry the 19th century was a time of extraordinary productivity. Two important new tools, electricity and spectroscopy, gave chemists new ways to manipulate and observe materials and transformed their science in the same way that the telescope had done for astronomy and the microscope for biology. The number of known elements nearly doubled. Mendeleyev's periodic table began to make sense of them and provided a working matrix for the great breakthroughs yet to come in both chemistry and physics at the turn of the century and in the early 1900s. The birth of organic chemistry opened up enormous industrial potential for applied chemistry, including the invention of new dyes and materials.

Most important at the outset, the birth (or rather rebirth) of atomic theory enabled Dalton, Avogadro, and those who followed to begin to make sense out of the rules of chemistry—how substances reacted and bonded with each other—as well as the properties of gases.

Of course not everyone was happy with atomism, either at the time Dalton first set it forth, or even later, at the end of the century. The highly influential physicist Ernst Mach (1838–1916) opposed atomism right up to the time of his death. It was one thing, he said, to observe that two volumes of hydrogen gas combined with one volume of oxygen gas to form water vapor; it was quite another to

Kekulé's benzene ring

postulate that two atoms of hydrogen, which could not be seen, combined with an invisible atom of oxygen to form a molecule of water, which also could not be seen. But atomism at the very least, most scientists conceded, provided an excellent model, which, with the use of notations symbolizing atoms and their inter-reactions, made discussions of chemistry much clearer.

Atomism also opened the way to one of the great key discoveries of the century: an understanding of the nature of heat and thermodynamics, an area that had been clouded by mystery for centuries.

3
Indestructible Energy

TWO GREAT FORCES TURNED WHEELS and intrigued minds of the 19th century: steam and electricity. At the start of the century all industry had been transformed by James Watt's steam engine, which also provided inspiration for the theoretical study of energy. By mid-century, transportation was also transformed, with all the major ports of England linked by steam railroads and some 30,000 miles of track crisscrossing the North American continent. By the end of the century, electricity had begun to light up the world and provide the productive power for industry.

Scientists who delved into the heart of these two great sources of power turned up a treasure trove of insights into nature that fed back into the technological development of western Europe, the British Isles, North America, and the entire world. The key, as Joseph Black and James Watt discovered in the previous century, was understanding heat, its nature, its behavior, and, most of all, thermodynamics—the study of how thermal energy converts to other forms of energy and vice versa.

Early Work

For most 18th-century chemists and physicists, heat was an invisible, "imponderable" (that is, weightless) fluid called "caloric." When ice melted, it lost caloric. When water froze, it gained caloric in a sort of chemical reaction between water and heat. The theory, sometimes known as the material theory of heat, seemed to work well as an explanation: If you place a hot object next to a cold one, the heat does seem to flow from one to the other, as if it were a fluid. Also matter expands when heated, as if some fluid were being added to it. Caloric seemed to make sense, so very few scientists saw any reason to challenge it.

Few, that is, except the American-born Bavarian elector Count Rumford (who left America to avoid prosecution for collaborating with the British during the Revolutionary War). He also picked up recruits among the younger generation of English scientists around 1800—including Humphry Davy and Thomas Young. Rumford had realized that the act of boring cannons with dull instruments should have produced less heat (releasing less caloric) than boring with sharp instruments; use of the sharp instruments should have released more caloric, since they abraded the material more effectively. In fact exactly the opposite was true. To explain this Rumford suggested that the heat must be a kind of motion. It was not an idea that caught on quickly.

But as the 19th century dawned, John Dalton's atomic theory began to add credence to the idea that there might be tiny, invisible particles capable of agitating in a balloon full of gas or a vat of water or a block of ice—moving faster if hot, slower if cold.

An idea along these lines, known as kinetic theory (*kinetic* means produced by motion), had been introduced by Daniel Bernoulli in 1738, but atoms and molecules were not really taken seriously at the time. A few other people also tried to propose it after Dalton, but they were unknowns and no one paid much attention.

French scientists, meanwhile, were working on the theoretical basis for Watt's steam engine. Watt, an engineer, and his Scottish and English scientist friends were practical hands-on doers, many of them self-educated. The French, with their École Polytechnique in Paris, were stronger at theoretical science, with a preference for the material theory of heat (caloric). Jean-Baptiste-Joseph Fourier (1768–1830), who had a strong influence on mathematical physics, published a paper, *Théorie analytique de la chaleur* (*Analytical Theory of Heat*, 1822), in which he presented a new method for mathematical analysis and was the first to state clearly that a scientific equation must involve a consistent set of units—an idea known as "Fourier's theorem." He also examined the flow of heat through solids and a theory of dimensions that Descartes had suggested. But Fourier had no interest in the mechanical force associated with heat, and, in fact, he thought that "dynamical theories" and "natural philosophy" occupied two different and unrelated realms.

In Germany, meanwhile, the kinetic theory of heat was gaining ground. Friedrich Mohr (1806–79), a pupil of the chemist Justus von Liebig, wrote in 1837:

> Besides the known fifty-four chemical elements there exists in nature only one agent more, and this is called force; it can under suitable conditions appear as motion, cohesion, electricity, light, beat, and magnet. . . . Heat is thus not a particular kind of matter, but an oscillatory motion of the smallest parts of bodies.

All these ideas circled around one central thought without quite landing on it. It was up to an avid experimentalist named James Joule to give the concept a quantitative value.

Joule's Measurement

James Prescott Joule (1818–89) was a fanatic about heat. He measured the heat of everything. Even on his honeymoon he measured the water temperature at the top of a waterfall he and his wife were visiting and compared it with the temperature of the water at the bottom.

In a classic experiment that he performed in 1847, Joule measured the temperature of a tank of water and then inserted a paddle wheel into the water. Then he spun the paddle wheel for a long time, resulting in a very gradual rise in the temperature of the water. Joule measured the amount of work done by the paddle wheel and the rise in water temperature; that is, he figured out how much mechanical energy produced how much heat, a value now known as the "mechanical equivalent of heat." Joule spent 10 years or more of his life

James Joule *(AIP Emilio Segrè Visual Archives)*

measuring the heat produced by every process he could think of—mechanical, electrical, or magnetic—and in every medium he could think of.

Others before Joule had tried to come up with a figure for the mechanical equivalent of heat. Rumford had done it but had come out way too high; Julius Robert Mayer (1814–78) also had figured it out but not as accurately as Joule. Joule's was the best figure up to his time, and he backed it up with voluminous experimental data. In his honor a unit of work or energy equal to 10 million ergs, or about a quarter of a calorie, is named a joule.

Joule's work led directly to the recognition of a fundamental principle known as the first law of thermodynamics, and for this he often shares the credit with the man who formulated it.

The First Law

So, to Lavoisier's principle of the indestructibility of matter, it was Hermann von Helmholtz (1821–94) who added a corollary law in 1847: "Nature as a whole possesses a store of energy which cannot in any wise be added to or subtracted from." The quantity of energy in the universe is as indestructible as the quantity of matter; matter cannot be created or destroyed, nor can energy. (Julius Robert Mayer had put forth a concept of the conservation of energy in 1842, before either Joule's work or Helmholtz's, but it was less completely supported by evidence than Helmholtz's.)

Known as the first law of thermodynamics, this idea is sometimes summed up as "You can't get something for nothing." Or, put still another way: You cannot get more energy out of a reaction than you put into it. That is:

Thermal energy input = useful energy + waste energy

As Black and Watt saw, a heat engine (of which Watt's steam engine was the first successful example) could convert thermal energy stored in gases into the kinetic energy of turbines and pistons. That is, since gases expand when heated, thermal energy stored in steam could be converted to motion. The original source of energy in such a system is the chemical potential energy of the fuel—wood or coal—that is used to produce steam.

The first law of thermo-dynamics is one of the most revolutionary ideas in the history of physical science, and according to science historian A. C. Crombie, "Its implications and the problems it posed dominated physics in the period between the electromagnetic researches of Faraday and Maxwell and the introduction of the quantum theory by Planck in 1900." It would also prove to need extension to include both energy and matter together with the advent of Einsteinian physics in the 20th century, when it became evident that energy can sometimes be converted to matter and vice versa.

Hermann von Helmholtz, one of the founders of the principle of conservation of energy, is also known for his contributions to ophthalmology, anatomy, and physiology. *(Courtesy of the National Library of Medicine)*

As James Clerk Maxwell wrote in a tribute to Helmholtz:

> To appreciate the scientific value of Helmholtz's little essay on the Conservation of Force, we should have to ask those to whom we owe the greatest discoveries in thermodynamics and other branches of modern physics, how many times they have read it over, and how often during their researches they felt the weighty statements of Helmholtz acting on their minds like an irresistible driving power.

In his later years Helmholtz became a mentor of Max Planck (1858–1947), the founder of quantum theory, and through Planck, Helmholtz's influence would also reach far forward into the 20th century.

The Second Law

Nicolas-Léonard Sadi Carnot (1796–1832), unlike Fourier, was a French engineer, and his approach was more practical. He likened the steam engine to a water wheel—a somewhat flawed analogy—and he initially put forth the idea that the boiler in a steam engine put out the same amount of heat as received by the condenser at the lower temperature, that no heat was lost. While this is not so, Carnot made the important link between the heat of the fire, the pressure of the steam, and the mechanical motion (or work) of the engine. He recognized that the energy output of an engine depended on the difference between the high temperature at the boiler and the lower temperature at the condenser and the amount of heat that passed between them. He speculated that the total energy of the universe was constant and only changed from one form to another. But Carnot died of cholera at the age of 36 before he had a chance to develop his ideas any further. His ideas were published in 1824 in his only work, *On the Motive Power of Fire,* but it had a considerable influence on those who followed.

German physicist Rudolf Clausius (1822–88) was not an experimentalist; his great gift lay in the ability to interpret and perform mathematical analysis of other scientists' results. Clausius came to the conclusion in 1850 that heat could not by itself pass from one body to another at a higher temperature. Considered to be another of the 19th century's major discoveries in physics, his formulation has become known as the second law of thermodynamics.

Rudolf Clausius cofounded the second law of thermodynamics in cooperation with Lord Kelvin. *(AIP Emilio Segrè Visual Archives, Physics Today Collection)*

Irish-born William Thomson (1824–1907) became known as Lord Kelvin of Largs in Scotland and is often referred to by either name. In addition to contributing to the dynamical theory of heat, he synthesized the ideas of Carnot and Joule in a paper published in 1851 on the convertibility of heat into mechanical energy, also a version of the second law of thermodynamics. For this contribution he is sometimes given some of the credit, alongside Clausius, for discovering the principle.

The second law of thermodynamics can be stated simply: You can't break even. Suppose a diver stands at the top of a cliff over a deep pool. At this moment the diver has gravitational potential energy. When he or she jumps, that energy is transformed to kinetic energy, which, in turn, is transferred to the water as thermal energy when the diver hits it. This process, by the way, does not reverse spontaneously (at least, not usually); energy transformations have a preferred direction. Although it would be

William Thomson, Lord Kelvin, was the other cofounder, with Rudolf Clausius, of the second law of thermodynamics. *(The Smithsonian Institution, AIP Emilio Segrè Visual Archives)*

possible to see the diver bounce back up to the top of the cliff, some kind of bungee cord or spring or a crane would be required to achieve the feat. Otherwise the diver will have to hike back up or hitch a ride in a dune buggy. Or, in another example, hot soup always becomes cold spontaneously, but cold soup does not become hot unless heat is applied from an outside source.

Another way of expressing the second law of thermodynamics is to say that in a closed system—one having no outside source of energy—entropy increases. Entropy is a measure of the disorder of a system: the greater the disorder, the higher the entropy. Also, because entropy tends to increase, thermal energy does not flow from cooler to warmer (molecules and atoms are more ordered in cooler solids than in warmer liquids and gases), and, in general, natural processes move toward greater disorder.

At one level this means that without the energy from the Sun, the Earth would soon run down. Eventually the Sun and, possibly, the universe will exhaust their resources and fizzle. Or, put another

Great Moments in Thermodynamics

1822

▶ Jean-Baptiste Joseph Fourier publishes equations of heat flow

1824

▶ Nicolas Léonard Sadi Carnot's theorem becomes the basis for the independent formulations of the second law of thermodynamics by Clausius and Kelvin

1847

▶ James Prescott Joule experimentally establishes the mechanical theory of heat (the "mechanical equivalent of heat")

▶ Hermann von Helmholtz outlines the first law of thermodynamics (the law of conservation of energy)

1850–51

▶ Rudolf Clausius and William Thomson (Lord Kelvin) formulate the second law of thermodynamics

ca. 1860–70

▶ James Clerk Maxwell and Ludwig Boltzmann independently develop the kinetic theory of gases

1871

▶ Maxwell's demon is presented in his *Theory of Heat*

way, no matter how much you straighten your room this week, you will have to straighten it again next week.

Kinetic Theory of Gases

The caloric theory of heat finally met its end around 1866, when James Clerk Maxwell (1831–79) and Ludwig Boltzmann (1844–1906) independently used a series of equations to describe the behavior of gases more completely than anyone ever had before. The temperature of a gas, Maxwell said, does not reflect the speed of movement of all the molecules of a gas uniformly. Instead it reflects the statistical average of their movement, in all directions and at all velocities. When a gas is heated, he explained, the molecules move faster and bump into each other more, and this bumping increases the pressure of the gas.

Maxwell's Demon

In 1871 Maxwell invented a tiny character—which has come to be known as Maxwell's demon—to illustrate the statistical nature of both entropy and his kinetic theory of heat in gases. Imagine a gas evenly distributed in both chambers of a two-room house. Only one opening exists, and that is a sliding door between the two rooms. As described in Maxwell's kinetic theory, some of the gas molecules in both rooms are moving slowly, while others are moving rapidly. As the molecules float (or speed) by, the demon grabs the slow ones and puts them in the other room. From the other room he grabs the fast molecules and pulls them through the opening into the first room. In this way, eventually, one room fills with cold (slow-moving) molecules and the other contains hot (fast-moving) molecules. If such a demon existed (of course it does not), you could heat a room without using any energy.

From the caloric theory of the 18th century, physics had come a long way in a little over 70 years of studying the nature of heat and its interrelations with other forms of energy. Based on the power of the atomic theory and through the use of mathematics, models, and careful experimentation, two abiding principles had been achieved that provided substantially greater insight into the workings of thermodynamics.

4
Magnetism, Electricity, and Light

ALL OF EUROPE WAS EXPERIMENTING with electrical current in 1819, when Hans Christian Ørsted began teaching his physics class at the University of Copenhagen. Ørsted was no exception. In a classroom demonstration, he took a wire through which he ran an electric current and brought it close to a compass needle. Speculation had been in the air for a long time that some relationship existed between electricity and magnetism. Ørsted probably suspected that the electrical current and the magnet would have some effect on each other. He was right.

With a sudden and immediate reaction, the compass needle swung, not in the direction of the current, which streamed steadily from Ørsted's voltaic cell, but instead into a position at a right angle to the current. Ørsted reversed the direction of the current. The compass needle swung again, this time in the opposite direction, again at a right angle.

Ørsted had demonstrated for the first time, before his students, that a connection exists between electricity and magnetism, and he opened the door to a new study: electromagnetism. It would prove to be the most productive area of study in the 19th century.

An Ancient Mystery

The study of both electricity and magnetism dated as far back as the work of William Gilbert of Colchester (1544–1603) in the 16th

William Gilbert explored the nature of magnetism in his work *De Magnete,* published in 1600. In this illustration from his book, a blacksmith magnetizes a glowing iron bar by pounding it with the ends pointing north (*septentrio*) and south (*auster*). (*Courtesy of the Burndy Library*)

century. While the ancient Greeks had known about the magnetic properties of amber, Gilbert showed that many other substances could be magnetized—sulfur, glass, iron—and he was the first to use the terms *electric force, electric attraction,* and *magnetic pole.* Often thought of as the founder of the study of electricity, he wrote about his researches in his book *De Magnete,* published in 1600.

In the 17th century Otto von Guericke devised a machine that could generate static electricity, and in 1745 both Pieter van Musschenbroek (1692–1761) and Ewald von Kleist (1700–48) independently discovered the principle of the Leyden jar. Both scientific and popular interest in electricity swelled, and American scientist and diplomat Benjamin Franklin (1706–90) did extensive research exploring the nature of its positive and negative polarity, its relationship with magnetism, its ability to melt metals, and so on. He also demonstrated, with his famous kite experiment, that lightning is electricity.

Not until Volta's invention of the voltaic cell (see chapter 1), though, did it become possible to create a continual, steady source of electricity; up to that point all sources of electricity were static. Before Volta, electricity could be stored, but it could only be discharged in a single (often mighty) jolt.

The big breakthroughs with electricity, however, still lay ahead in the 19th century. Not only would electricity, once harnessed, change the way people lived, but from a new understanding of electricity, magnetism, and their relationship would emerge powerful new theories that would transform the way people thought about the universe. A young man named Michael Faraday took the first giant steps in this direction.

Faraday, The Great Experimenter

One of the most admirable and honorable figures in the history of science, Michael Faraday had neither the education nor the leisure time

Michael Faraday's skills as an experimenter laid the groundwork for many key 19th-century breakthroughs. *(AIP Emilio Segrè Visual Archives, E. Scott Barr Collection)*

that many of his contemporary colleagues enjoyed. One of 10 children of a blacksmith in England, Michael Faraday (1791–1867) started life with no hope of going to school beyond learning to read and write, much less obtaining a university education. At the age of 12, he began earning his share of the rent, and his school days were finished. But some people have such curious minds that nothing can keep them from trying to find out what the world is made of, or why people act the way they do, or what makes things work. Michael Faraday had one of those tirelessly curious minds. He also had a bit of luck: He found a job as an apprentice to a bookbinder, and as he bound the outside of the books, he avidly devoured the words inside. He read the articles on electricity in the *Encyclopaedia Britannica* and Lavoisier's *Traité élémentaire de chimie* (*Elements of Chemistry*). He also read (and bound) a book called *Conversations on Chemistry*, by Jane Marcet, whose popularization of chemistry was widely read in the early 1800s, when it was published.

Then another piece of luck came Faraday's way. A customer of the bookbinder gave Faraday tickets to four lectures by Humphry Davy at the Royal Institution. Faraday was elated and took scrupulous notes at all four lectures, which he later bound and sent to Davy, with an application for a position as assistant at the institution. A few months later, when an opening came up, Davy offered the job to Faraday. "Let him wash bottles," one of Davy's colleagues said. "If he is any good, he will accept the work, if he refuses, he is not good for anything." The job paid less than Faraday's bookbinding job, but he jumped at the chance.

Shortly thereafter, in 1813, Davy set off for Europe with Faraday at his side as secretary and scientific assistant. Though Davy's wife treated Faraday as a servant, the young man never complained, instead taking advantage of the opportunity to meet the key figures of science, including Volta, Ampère, Gay-Lussac, Arago, Humboldt, and Cuvier. As they traveled from laboratory to laboratory across Europe, performing experiments and attending lectures, Faraday received the education he had never had.

On their return, in 1815, Faraday became, officially, assistant in the laboratory and mineral collection and superintendent of the apparatus at the Royal Institution. He was Davy's right hand in the laboratory, adroit, expert, and dedicated, often working from nine o'clock in the morning until eleven at night. After a few months he received a raise to £100 a year, and he remained at that salary until 1853.

When Faraday read of Ørsted's experiment in 1820, he—like the rest of the scientific community—became very excited. Ørsted's compass showed that electric current was not traversing the wire end to end in a straight line, as everyone had supposed, but instead was circling the wire. Further demonstrations by André-Marie Ampère [ahm-PAIR] in Paris corroborated this idea. Ampère showed that if two electrical wires are strung parallel, with one loose enough to move freely, when the current in both wires runs in the same direction, the wires are drawn together; when the current runs in opposite directions, the two wires are pushed apart.

Jane Marcet, Science Writer

One of the world's first female science writers, Jane Marcet (1769–1858) completed *Conversations in Chemistry* in 1805, which saw its first publication in 1806 and was already in its second edition by 1807. Many other editions would follow—a total of 16 British editions, two French editions, and some 16 or more in the United States—making it the most popular chemistry book of the early 1800s.

Born Jane Haldimand, she was the daughter of wealthy, enlightened parents who provided her the same education that at the time would ordinarily have been reserved for their male offspring. Young Jane had excellent tutors in a broad range of subjects including not only the traditional feminine pursuits of dancing, painting, and music but also mathematics, philosophy, and astronomy.

At age 30 Jane Haldimand married Alexander Marcet, a Swiss doctor and a respected professor of medicine. The Marcets became part of a fashionable and elite circle of London society that included many scientists. Soon Jane Marcet began writing about the cutting edge of science for young people—including the mechanisms of Watt's steam engine, as well as the work of Davy, Lavoisier, Cavendish, and Black. As the title of her book implies, it was built around imaginary conversations about chemistry—not between scientists, though, but between a knowledgeable older woman (Mrs. Brian, known as "Mrs. B.") and two young women, Caroline and Emily.

Marcet's Mrs. B. made use of illustrations and experiments to encourage her young friends to think for themselves. On the subject of heat radiation, for example, Mrs. B. remarks, "Before I conclude the subject . . . I must observe . . . that different surfaces [give off heat] in different

Faraday set up a simple experiment of his own. In September 1821 he demonstrated "electromagnetic rotation," showing that a wire could be made to move around a fixed magnet through the use of electric current, and that a magnet could be made to move around a fixed wire. It was the first primitive electric motor.

Unfortunately Davy became angry with Faraday over this experiment, claiming that Faraday had overheard a discussion between Davy and William Wollaston describing a similar experiment. Fara-

degrees." "These surfaces are all the same temperature?" queries Emily. "Undoubtedly," supplies Mrs. B. To illustrate the point she shows Caroline and Emily a cube made of tin having a different texture on each of its four surfaces—a polished side, a sooty side, a rusty side, and a sanded side. After bringing all four sides to the same temperature by filling the cube with hot water, Mrs. B. uses a mirror to reflect the heat radiated from each side onto a thermometer. Her students can see the four different readings, and, along with Marcet's readers, they get the point. Not only did Faraday find this book absorbing, but countless other adult readers concurred with him. The book was so popular that Marcet went on to write about other subjects, including *Conversations on Natural Philosophy* (1819), *Conversations on Mineralogy* in (1829), and *Evidences of Christianity*, in which she explored the historic credibility of the New Testament.

Jane Marcet's book for young adults, *Conversations on Chemistry,* probably helped interest young Faraday in pursuing a career in science. *(Edgar Fahs Smith Collection—University of Pennsylvania Library)*

day admitted he may have gotten a start from the conversation, but his apparatus was substantially different, and both Wollaston and history seem to agree on this point.

In any case, it is perhaps the least of Faraday's discoveries. He was stalking a much bigger conquest. In 1822 Faraday wrote in his notebook: "Convert magnetism into electricity." Ørsted had used electricity to create magnetism (the compass needle responds to magnetic force); might not the reverse process also take place?

Faraday started off from ideas already set forth in part by Ampère and another physicist, William Sturgeon. He began with an iron ring, wrapping one segment of it with a coil of wire. He could intro-

Michael Faraday in his laboratory at the Royal Institution *(AIP Emilio Segrè Visual Archives)*

duce an electric current into the wire by closing a circuit with a key. He then wrapped another segment of the ring with wire and connected it to a galvanometer. He thought that the current in the first coil of wire might cause a current in the second coil. The galvanometer would measure the presence of the second current and tell the story.

This idea did work—it was the first transformer—but the results contained a surprise. Despite the steady magnetic force set up in the iron ring, no steady electric current ran through the second coil. Instead a flash of current ran through the second coil when Faraday closed the circuit—with a jump on the galvanometer. Then, when he opened the circuit again, another flash of current was marked by a second galvanometer jump.

Since Faraday knew no mathematics (having never gone to school), he used visualization to explain this phenomenon—and came up with the idea of lines of magnetic force. He had noticed that if you sprinkled a paper with iron filings, held it over a strong magnet, and tapped it, the filings would arrange themselves in distinct patterns, along what Faraday concluded were the magnet's lines of force. He conceived of the idea that an electric current forms a kind of magnetic field radiating out in all directions from its source. When he closed the circuit in his experiment, lines of force radiated out, but the second coil of wire cut across them. When that happened, a current was induced in the second coil. When he opened the circuit, the lines of force "collapsed back," and again the second wire cut through their path and a current was induced. He saw how he could work out what the lines of force would look like for a bar magnet, for a spherical magnet such as the Earth, and for an electric wire. For the first time since Galileo and Newton had conceived of the mechanistic universe, now a new and even more productive way to look at the universe—field theory—was in the making.

During one of the many enormously popular lectures he was now giving at the Royal Institution, in 1831, Faraday demonstrated the lines of force in another way. He took a coil of wire and moved a magnet into the coil. The needle of the galvanometer attached to the wire swung, then stopped when the movement of the magnet stopped. When he moved the magnet out of the coil, again the galvanometer registered. Moving the magnet around inside the coil registered. If he moved the coil of wire over the magnet, the presence of a current showed up. But if he let the magnet just sit motionless inside the coil of wire, no action registered on the galvanometer; there was no current. Faraday had discovered the principle of electromagnetic induction. That is, he had found that by combining mechanical motion with magnetism he could produce electric current. This was the basic principle of the electric generator or dynamo. (Another physicist, Joseph Henry, across the Atlantic Ocean in the United States, had also come up with an excellent demonstration of this same idea, but he had put it aside without publishing. As a result Faraday, who pursued his work with extraordinary single-mindedness, gets the credit, which Henry freely acknowledged.)

Faraday's next step, of course, was to build a generator, producing a continuous source of electricity instead of the jerky, on-off variety he had induced in his experiment. This he did by setting up a copper wheel so that its edge passed between the poles of a permanent magnet. As long as the wheel turned, an electric current was set up in it, and the current could be led off and set to work. By adding a water wheel or steam engine to turn the wheel, the kinetic energy of falling water or the combustive energy of burning fuel could be transformed to electrical power. Electrical generators today do not look much like Faraday's original model, and it took some 50 years for practical applications to be found, but it was unquestionably the most important electrical discovery ever made.

From childhood Faraday had a profound belief in the interconnection and unity of natural forces and phenomena, and he recognized that his field theory, which he first published in 1844, and his explorations of the interrelatedness of magnetism, electricity, and motion contributed to this vision. In the opening paragraph of his paper "On the Magnetization of Light and the Illumination of Magnetic Lines of Force," read before the Royal Society on November 5, 1845, he wrote:

> I have long held an opinion, almost amounting to conviction, in common I believe with many other lovers of natural knowledge, that the various forms under which the forces of matter are made manifest have one common origin; or, in other words, are so directly related and mutually dependent, that they are convertible, as it were, one into another, and possess equivalents of power in their action.

At first not many people took Faraday's field theory seriously, but in many ways Faraday's belief in the fundamental unity of nature was vindicated by the work of Joule, Thomson, Helmholtz, Clausius, and Maxwell in the following decades.

Meanwhile the relationship between Faraday and Davy had continued to deteriorate. As time passed Davy must have recognized that Faraday was passing him up, and he began to become jealous and bitter. When Faraday's name came up for admission as a fellow to the Royal Society, Davy opposed it; but Faraday was made a fellow in 1824, despite Davy's lone dissenting vote. In 1825 Faraday became director of the laboratory, and he became professor of chemistry at the Royal Institution in 1833. A gentle and religious man, who preferred to spend time in his laboratory or at home in the companionship of his wife, Sarah Barnard, Faraday never responded to Davy's shabby behavior. He had other things to do. As his successor at the Royal Institution, John Tyndall, described him, Faraday "was a man of excitable and fiery nature; but through high self-discipline he had converted the fire into a central glow and motive power of life, instead of permitting it to waste itself in useless passion."

To Faraday, the great experimentalist, we owe a giant debt. As British physicist Ernest Rutherford said in 1931:

> The more we study the work of Faraday with the perspective of time, the more we are impressed by his unrivalled genius as an experimenter and a natural philosopher. When we consider the magnitude and extent of his discoveries and their influence on the progress of science and industry, there is no honour too great to pay to the memory of Michael Faraday—one of the greatest discoverers of all time.

The Scottish Theorist

James Clerk [pronounced CLARK] Maxwell was born in 1831, the year Michael Faraday made his most influential discovery, electromagnetic induction. As a child Maxwell was so brilliant in mathematics that he did not seem to have good sense: His classmates called him Daffy. At 15 he submitted to the Royal Society of Edinburgh a paper on the drawing of oval curves that was so impressive that many members of the society thought it could not have been

Thomas Alva Edison (1847–1931)

Thomas Edison was not very interested in science. He did not care much about the nature of electricity—that was for the scientists to figure out. What he wanted to do was tame it and make it jump through hoops. He wanted to put it to work—a word that could have served as Edison's middle name. Born in Ohio to poor parents, Edison was taken out of school by his mother at an early age, and by age 12 he had found a job as a newsboy selling newspapers on a train traveling across Michigan. Not content simply to sell papers, he started publishing his own onboard the train as it made its passenger run between Port Huron and Detroit. Newspapers were not Edison's primary interest, though, and he put his profits into buying chemicals and setting up a small laboratory in the train's baggage car. This chemical work came to a sudden end, though, when one of his experiments caused an explosion that nearly wrecked the baggage car, and both the young experimenter and his chemicals were hastily kicked off at the next stop.

By 1862 his interest had shifted to the new field of telegraphy and his reputation as the fastest and most accurate telegrapher in the country earned him enough money to begin collecting books on electricity, including the collected works of Michael Faraday. His next venture, in 1869, found him in New York, where he offered his first major invention, an improved stock-ticker, to a big Wall Street firm. He wanted $5,000 for it, but before he could ask his price, the president of the firm told him he could not offer more than $40,000! Edison took it. By the time he was 23, he was solidly in the inventing business with his own small firm of consulting engineers.

Edison usually put in 20 hours a day at this work and by 1876 had expanded his interests to set up a research laboratory in Menlo Park, New Jersey. There his true genius flowered. Out of his so-called invention factory, the world's first full-scale private research facility, a steady stream of new inventions soon flowed. Working with a staff of engineers (numbering more than 80 at its peak), the "Wizard of Menlo Park" patented more than 1,300 inventions before he died. Not always the most likable of men, brusque to friends and ruthless to his competitors, he nevertheless was responsible for an amazing number of electric inventions and products that changed the lifestyle of the world—including the phonograph in 1877 and the incandescent electric lamp in 1879. The following year he illuminated the main street of Menlo Park with electric lights to the astonishment of reporters from around the world. In 1881, at a location on Pearl Street, New York, he built the world's first central electrical power station. In the 1890s Edison began making America's first commercial motion pictures using his Kinetoscope process, and he began showing the films, which could only be viewed in a small viewing machine by one person at a time, in a "Kinetoscope Parlor" in New York in 1894.

Edison died in 1931, one of the most famous inventors of all time. In 1960 he was elected to the Hall of Fame for Great Americans, a tribute not only to his major inventions but also to the hundreds of others, large and small, that, in the words of the United States Congress, forever "revolutionized civilization."

Thomas Alva Edison (left) in his lab. (With him is German-American electrical engineer Charles Steinmetz.) *(General Electric Research Laboratory, courtesy of AIP Emilio Segrè Visual Archives)*

James Clerk Maxwell, whose electromagnetic theory transformed the study of physics *(AIP Emilio Segrè Visual Archives)*

written by someone so young. By the time Maxwell was in his early 30s, he had already explained the probable nature of Saturn's rings (1857), about which he was right, and had developed, independently of Ludwig Boltzmann, the kinetic theory of gases (1866).

But he had always been intrigued by Faraday's work; in December 1855 and February 1856, as a 24-year-old fellow at Trinity College, Cambridge, Maxwell had presented an extraordinary paper entitled "Faraday's Lines of Force." Now, between 1864 and 1873, Maxwell would bring his mathematical wizardry to bear on Faraday's speculations about electromagnetic lines of force, providing the theoretical justification they needed.

In the process Maxwell worked out a series of simple equations that described all the observations made about both magnetism and electricity and illustrated that the two forces were inextricably bound together. This monumental work, known as the electromagnetic theory, showed that magnetism and electricity could not exist separately.

In support of Faraday's field theory, Maxwell showed that an electromagnetic field was, in fact, created by the oscillation of an electrical current. This field, he added, radiated outward from its source at a constant speed. This constant speed could be calculated by taking a ratio of certain magnetic units to certain electrical units, which worked out to be approximately 186,300 miles per second. Light travels at 186,282 miles per second—a coincidence too astounding, Maxwell thought, to be accidental. From this he came to the conclusion that light itself must be an oscillating electric charge. Light, he concluded, was electromagnetic radiation! This point he was unable to prove, but it seemed a strong hunch—and his hunch was proved a generation later.

But Maxwell went further. Light, he postulated, was probably just one of a large family of radiations caused by charges oscillating at different velocities. (Evidence had already been found that there might be a lot more than we would see: William Herschel had discovered infrared light, invisible to the naked eye, in 1800; Johann Ritter had found ultraviolet light, also invisible, at the other end of the spectrum in 1801.)

Maxwell published his *Treatise on Electricity and Magnetism*, on his theory of electromagnetism, in 1873. It was a brilliant work, adding the precision of mathematics and quantitative prediction to Faraday's views on field theory and, specifically, on electromagnetism. Like Thomas Young, he postulated the existence of ether throughout space as the medium through which electromagnetic waves traveled; this postulation was later disproved, but his equations do not depend on ether's existence, and they hold up as well as ever in the everyday world of "classical" physics (though not in Einstein's physics of relativity or the world of quantum mechanics).

In one of those strange coincidences of history, James Clerk Maxwell died in 1879, the same year that another great theoretician, Albert Einstein, was born. Like Maxwell's work in the 19th century, Einstein's would dominate physics from the beginning of the 20th century to the present. Maxwell did not live long enough to see his theories validated experimentally (he died of cancer before he was 50), but the proof was not far off. Less than a decade later, a young physicist in a laboratory in Germany did the job.

Hertz's Waves

A student of Helmholtz, Heinrich Rudolf Hertz (1857–94) became interested in Maxwell's equations concerning electromagnetic fields in 1883. Helmholtz suggested that Hertz try for a prize offered by the Berlin Academy of Science for work in electromagnetics, and Hertz, by now teaching at Karlsruhe, decided to give it a try. In 1888 he found something. Hertz set up an experiment that made it possible for him to detect the presence of the type of long-wave radiation that would be produced if light were in fact a type of electromagnetic radiation. He also devised a way to measure the shape of the wave if it appeared.

Young, Fresnel, and Light Waves

Light, nearly everyone knew, was made of particles—or at least so they thought. Newton had established that long ago. For one thing light could not pass around corners, as sound waves could, and light cast sharp shadows. So when English physicist Thomas Young (1773–1829) began to think that light might be a wave instead, he had a sharp uphill battle to fight.

The wave versus particle controversy was age-old, though. (Francesco Grimaldi, 1618–63, had observed that a beam of light passed through two narrow apertures became slightly wider than the apertures, indicating a slight bend, which he called "diffraction.") Some people believed the jury was still out on the issue.

As a child Thomas Young was a remarkable prodigy who began reading at age two, read the Bible twice by the age of six, and learned a dozen languages, including Persian and Swahili. In later life this tremendous facility with language served him well when in 1814 he tackled deciphering the hieroglyphics of the ancient Rosetta Stone found by Napoleon's expedition to Egypt in 1799.

Early in his career Young lectured from 1801 to 1803, with Davy, at Rumford's Royal Institution, and during these years he investigated the anatomy of the eye (finding that astigmatism is caused by imperfections in the cornea), color theory (founding, with Helmholtz, the Young—Helmholtz three-color theory that later became the basis for color television and color photography), and the nature of light.

To test the particle-versus-wave question, Young performed a test, sometimes known as his "fringe experiment," in which he shined a light through several narrow openings. At the edge of these openings, several blurred bands of light appeared. If light were particles and not waves, only a clear, sharp shadow should have appeared. Particle theory had no explanation for this new demonstration of light diffraction. Then Young went further. He thought about the way two pitches of sound sometimes cancel each other out. (An especially good example is the way two sounds on a public amplification system may start out together, screeching loudly, and then suddenly produce nothing but silence.) The reason for this is that two different pitches of sounds travel in waves of different length. They may start together with the peaks of the waves matched, then get out of sync so that the trough of one coincides with the peak of the other, and they cancel each other, producing no sound. Young thought that if light were produced by waves as well, the same kind of interference might occur. Young projected light beams through two narrow openings and shined them on a wall. The two beams overlapped, and where they overlapped, stripes of light and dark appeared, indicating that interference existed for light exactly as it did for sound. Thomas Young had resurrected the wave theory of light.

Young also suggested that light traveled in transverse waves—that is, at right angles to the point from which it emanated, much the way waves of water do in the ocean—not in longitudinal waves as sound does. This idea helped resolve some questions about polarized light and double refraction, and it also had implications, once Maxwell's theory of electromagnetism was established, for the entire electromagnetic spectrum, of which light is only a part.

Initially most scholars laughed at Young's wave theory. It remained for Augustin Fresnel, in France, to provide the needed mathematical backup. But light-wave theory still had problems. If light consisted of waves, not particles, then the waves had to travel in some medium, such as the air provides for sound waves and water provides for waves in the ocean. (There is no air outside the atmosphere to transmit light from stars.) Early wave theorists—including Maxwell much later in the century—thought there must be an "ether" filling all space, through which light undulated, but no proof of that ether's existence had ever been found. Meanwhile, though, more and more scientists turned to the wave theory, light still seemed to behave sometimes as if composed of particles. Albert Michelson and Edward Morley would show in 1887 that the suspected ether did not exist, and the continuing question of light's nature led to some of the most profound discoveries of the next century.

Thomas Young resurrected the wave theory of light. *(Edgar Fahs Smith Collection— University of Pennsylvania Library)*

It did appear and he was able to measure it. The wavelength was 2.2 feet (66 centimeters)—one million times the size of a wavelength of visible light. Hertz was able to show, as well, that the waves he measured involved both electric and magnetic fields and therefore had an electromagnetic nature.

What Hertz had found were not light waves, but, as it turned out, radio waves, for which Marchese Guglielmo Marconi found a use in 1894 as a kind of wireless communication. (*Radio* is short for

Babbage, Lovelace, and the First Computers

As 19th-century discoveries about electricity and magnetism opened one door after another, soon spawning electric lights, electric motors, and ultimately thousands of inventions, two individuals working together were still far ahead of their time. Charles Babbage (1792–1871) was an ingenious British inventor and mathematician. Born in Devonshire he attended the University of Cambridge and became a founding member of the Royal Astronomical Society. He also helped establish the Analytical Society and Statistical Society, and he became a fellow of the Royal Society in 1816. Given his interests in statistics and mathematics and his talent as an inventor, he began working on a design for a "Difference Engine" to perform complicated calculations quickly and automatically.

Meanwhile Ada Byron, countess of Lovelace (1815–52) and daughter of the British poet Lord Byron, had grown up with a keen interest in mathematics. Self-taught in geometry she also learned from whatever sources were available to her, including friends, tutors, and classes in astronomy and math. She and Babbage met in 1833 and these two individuals with a passion for numbers began collaborating. The Difference Engine was a mechanical device—not electrical—but it relied on programming concepts and had a complex design capable of handling extensive and involved calculations. Lovelace showed a ready understanding of the concept of a programmed machine when she translated and annotated a paper written in French about Babbage's Difference Engine. Money for the project ran out, though, and Babbage and Lovelace never saw it work. However, in 1991 a team of computer experts carefully followed Babbage's design notes and drawings and found that

radiotelegraphy—that is telegraphy by radiation rather than telegraphy by electric currents.)

Hertz had succeeded in proving the existence of electromagnetic waves, verifying the validity of Maxwell's equations. Another piece of the great puzzle of physics slipped into place.

Throughout the 19th century, a new pattern had begun to emerge in physics, a pattern of an idea set forth, validated by experiment, and reinforced by mathematical theory. It was a three-

---

the design was sound and the Babbage Difference Engine they produced ran perfectly.

Lovelace and Babbage also collaborated on another machine—the Analytical Engine, which is considered the first attempt at a modern digital computer. The machine was designed to read data from a stack of punched cards—much as early digital computers did—and it could store the data and perform calculations. Byron worked on writing the instructions, or programming, recorded by punching the cards—and she therefore receives recognition as the first computer programmer. The technology was not yet available, though, to make Babbage's Analytical Engine work. Yet the designs and the programming concepts laid groundwork for today's world of computers, from hand-held digital organizers to PCs to giant, number-crunching mainframe computers.

In 1979 the U.S. Department of Defense honored Lovelace's contributions to computer programming by giving the name Ada to its high-level, universal programming language.

Ada Byron, countess of Lovelace, was the first computer programmer. (*Stock Montage, Inc.*)

Heinrich Hertz succeeded in proving the existence of electromagnetic waves, verifying the validity of Maxwell's equations. *(Deutsches Museum, AIP Niels Bohr Library)*

fold process that increasingly gained the respect of the scientific community, and it worked for Mayer and Joule's heat equivalent; for Faraday, Maxwell, and Hertz's work on electromagnetism; and for Young and Fresnel's insights into the nature of light.

The most stunning accomplishment of the century was the steady untangling of threads by many hands—and the extraordinary genius of Faraday and Maxwell—that led to recognition of that great underlying force electromagnetism. Faraday's electric motor, transformer, and generator touch nearly every phase of our lives. But the significance of the underlying concepts of field theory and electromagnetism count among the most telling insights in the history of humankind's investigation into the nature of the universe.

5
Sky and Earth

FOR AS FAR BACK AS WE have records, people have been watching the skies, trying to understand the specks of light they saw above the night horizon. By the 19th century, theory had come a long way since Copernicus published his realization that the Sun, not Earth, resided at the center of the solar system; since Kepler published his work on orbits in 1609; and Kant worked on nebulae in the 18th century.

The telescope, first used for astronomy by Galileo in about 1610, gave a giant boost to the study of the universe. Now astronomers could make out the four great moons of Jupiter, the rings of Saturn, and the surface of the Moon. By the 18th century, thanks to improvements in the telescope, William Herschel discovered a seventh planet, Uranus, the first to be sighted since ancient times. Uranus's orbit was strange, however. This distant wanderer seemed to indicate by its movements that at least one more planet existed in the solar system. But where was it?

Other questions hovered in astronomers' minds. What were the cloudlike features cataloged so extensively by Charles Messier in the 18th century? Were they vast star systems, perhaps so far away that they appeared in the telescope as only a blur? Or were they just clouds of gas, as some supposed? How could anyone tell? What was the Sun made of? What about the stars?

Better detection methods lay at the heart of further progress. Greater precision was called for, as well as improved calculations and better instruments. To the challenge of these demands rose numerous dedicated, passionate, and incisive minds. But in the 19th

Maria Mitchell,
The First U.S. Woman Astronomer

Maria Mitchell was born in Nantucket, Massachusetts, in 1818. She had little opportunity for a formal education, but she was lucky enough to have a father who taught her, and she became the librarian at the Nantucket Atheneum. But she also learned to love watching the skies and made many amateur observations.

Then, on October 1, 1847, Maria Mitchell discovered a comet. She was 29. Immediately she gained the attention of the scientific community, and in 1849 she obtained a position at the U.S. Nautical Almanac Office. There she made astronomical computations and earned a reputation for her competence and accuracy. In 1865 she was named professor of astronomy at the newly formed Vassar College, a college for women.

Maria Mitchell's early contribution to the idea of women as professional scientists was a landmark. She succeeded in cutting through the prejudice of her time by doing what she loved, a profession thought to be alien or unsuited for women. Despite society's expectations that women should stay in the home, keep house, and raise children, Mitchell pursued a lifetime dedication to astronomy. She became the first woman admitted to the prestigious American Academy of Arts and Sciences, and until her death in 1889, she continued to teach other women at Vassar that science is for everyone, a point that her life work continues to make today.

Maria Mitchell was the first professional woman astronomer in the United States. *(Photo courtesy of Virginia Barney; print courtesy of H. Wright)*

century, two other unusual advances boosted results dramatically for astronomers: a way, surprisingly enough, to determine what elements the stars were made of (through spectroscopy) and a way to record what their telescopes pointed at (through photography, invented in 1826).

Seeing Better

An extraordinary proportion of advances in astronomy in the 19th century can be traced to the optical shop of one dedicated "lens grinder," a man whose name comes up whenever chemistry or physics or astronomy of this era is discussed: Joseph von Fraunhofer. Not only, as described earlier, did this once-penniless orphan boy grow up to discover the spectral lines that bear his name, but he was known far and wide for his precision-ground lenses and supremely crafted telescopes encased in red Moroccan leather.

Using one of Fraunhofer's telescopes, German astronomer Friedrich Bessel (1784–1846) made the first successful measurement of distance to a star, an object known as star number 61 in the constellation Cygnus (61 Cygni). For three centuries astronomers had been trying to determine the parallax of a star—any star. By finding the parallax (an object's apparent shift in position viewed from two different locations), an astronomer could make use of triangulation to determine the star's distance from Earth. But stars were so far away that, even measuring from six months apart on the Earth's orbit—which is the largest baseline available to earthbound astronomers—no good measurement had ever been made. Bessel chose 61 Cygni, even though it is a relatively dim star, because of its rapid proper motion (the apparent speed at which a star moves against a fixed background)—the most rapid of any star. He trained his trusty Fraunhofer on it, using a special instrument called a heliometer designed by Bessel and made by Fraunhofer. Through painstaking observations, Bessel measured the tiny displacements made by 61 Cygni and was able to compare its position with two other, even fainter, stars close by. To his amazement, 61 Cygni's parallax indicated that it was six light-years away (or six times the distance light can travel in one year—six times about 6 trillion miles.) Since Kepler had estimated that the stars were about a tenth of a light-year away and Newton had thought the distance was about two light-years, this discovery began to change astronomers' ideas drastically about the size of the universe.

Edward Emerson Barnard *(© UC Regents; Lick Observatory image)*

When Bessel announced his achievement in 1838, one more piece of the Copernican puzzle slipped into place, since even a small parallax for a star indicated that Earth was moving through space.

Also, with his heliometer, Bessel noticed that two stars, Sirius and Procyon, each had small deviations that could not be accounted for as parallactic but were more like wobbles. In 1841 Bessel postulated that each of these two stars was revolving around an unseen companion.

The rest of the story belongs to a second precision lens maker, Alvan Clark (1832–97) of Massachusetts, who, like Fraunhofer, made world-renowned lenses. One night in 1862 Clark was testing an 18-inch lens he and his father were working on, when he trained on Sirius and spotted a tiny speck of light nearby. It was the companion star whose existence Bessel had suggested 21 years before.

Two additional major discoveries were made with Clark telescopes. In 1877, during a close approach of Mars, Asaph Hall (1829–1907) of Connecticut, at the insistence of his wife (and former mathematics teacher), Angelina Stickney, to "try just one more night," discovered the two moons of Mars. Then in 1892 Edward Emerson Barnard (1857–1923), discovered a fifth moon of Jupiter, the first to be discovered in three centuries.

William Parsons, the third earl of Rosse, also made important discoveries—using his own giant 72-inch reflector telescope, known as the Leviathan, which he began building in 1842 by himself on the grounds of his estate in Ireland. By 1845 he was finished and ready to begin observing. Despite the constant foggy weather of his homeland, in 1848 Lord Rosse was able to study the Crab Nebula, which he named, and he identified several spiral-shaped objects that turned out to be very far-off galaxies. His telescope remained the largest in the world for 72 years.

Meanwhile Fraunhofer and Clark's success with improved lenses inspired the construction of several giant refractor telescopes at the end of the century, including one at the Lick Observatory in California, built in 1888, with a 36-inch aperture; and one at the Yerkes Observatory near Chicago, the construction of which Clark supervised. The Yerkes refractor, which opened in 1897, is still actively used by astronomers and, with its 40-inch aperture, remains the largest refractor telescope ever built.

Missing Planets

When the ancients looked at the skies, they saw certain objects they called "wanderers," or planets, that traveled in a strange manner across the canopy above, and they named them Mercury, Venus, Mars, Jupiter, and Saturn. Of the planets we know today, of course, they also

Joseph Le Verrier, the discoverer of Neptune, the eighth planet *(Courtesy of Yerkes Observatory)*

knew Earth, although no one at that time yet thought of *terra firma* as a planet. William Herschel astonished everyone by discovering Uranus in 1781. (He was not the first to see it, actually. It can be seen without binoculars or a telescope. But he was the first to identify that it was a planet.) Herschel had used systematic searching, a good telescope, excellent eyesight, and the help of his sister Caroline.

But perhaps there were more planets. Many astronomers were disturbed by an aberration in the orbit of Mercury, and Urbain-Jean-Joseph Le Verrier (1811–77) became sure that the presence of another planet between Mercury and the Sun would account for it. He made calculations and predicted its orbit and size (1,000 meters in diameter) and named it Vulcan. But, though many astronomers tried, no one ever found it. (Einstein would later explain why Mercury's orbit did not fit with Newtonian physics—despite the absence of another planet.)

Uranus's orbit had much the same problem, and with this Le Verrier had much better luck. Again he ran mathematical calculations and drew up equations. Then he contacted Johann Galle (1812–1910) in Berlin and told him where to look, and on September 23, 1846, they were in luck. Almost exactly where Le Verrier had said to look, Galle found the planet Neptune, another gaseous giant of nearly the same size as Uranus. The discovery was a triumph for astronomy as a science.

As we have seen before, more than one scientist may be hot on a trail, and some of the glory of being first can be a matter of luck. In the case of Neptune, John Couch Adams at Cambridge had made the same calculations a few months before Galle's discovery—but had not had access to a telescope to test out his thesis.

Fraunhofer's Lines

When Fraunhofer died at 39 on June 7, 1826, he left behind a legacy not only of his exquisite lenses but also his mysterious lines. Then in 1859, Gustav Kirchhoff and Robert Bunsen announced the invention of their spectroscope, opening up the discovery of numerous elements.

One evening Kirchhoff and Bunsen had been working in their laboratory in Heidelberg when they saw a fire burning in the nearby city of Mannheim, 10 miles away. They trained their spectroscope on it and discovered that they could detect the presence of barium and strontium from the arrangement of the fire's spectral lines—even at such a distance. Would it be possible, Bunsen began to wonder, to train the spectroscope on the light of the Sun and detect what elements were present there? "But people would think we were mad to dream of such a thing," he muttered.

In 1861 Kirchhoff put the idea to the test, and in the light from the Sun he succeeded in identifying nine elements: sodium, calcium, magnesium, iron, chromium, nickel, barium, copper, and zinc. Amazingly enough, the great source of light in the sky, once worshipped by ancient peoples as a god, contained many of the very same elements as the Earth. Gustav Kirchhoff had opened the door to two new sciences—spectroscopy and astrophysics—and had established another link between physics and chemistry on Earth and the physics and chemistry that ruled the stars. It was another stunning example of the convergence of worlds that once had seemed entirely separate.

William Huggins (© UC Regents; Lick Observatory image)

An English amateur astronomer named Sir William Huggins first put the spectroscope to use on deep-sky objects in 1864. A wealthy man, he had a private obser-

Mary Somerville, Scientist-Writer

It was not easy for women to open the doors of science in the 19th century. Mary Somerville (nee Fairfax) (1780–1872) not only opened them for herself but became the favorite science writer of such scientific greats as geologist Charles Lyell and astronomer John Herschel. The daughter of a Scottish admiral, Mary had no schooling until she was 10 and did not even read until she was 11, but she had not wasted even those early years. She collected fossils and stones and somehow got hold of a celestial globe and began to study astronomy.

As soon as she learned to read, doors opened even wider as she taught herself Latin and Greek. Taking time also to learn to play the piano, she approached her music with more than traditional drawing room art, even learning to tune the instrument and repairing broken strings herself.

Her earliest real love, though, was mathematics. She discovered algebra and geometry on her own and quickly mastered the writings of Euclid. Needless to say, all this intellectual and artistic activity was a little disconcerting to those around her—enough so that she was talked into marrying a rather stuffy and traditional friend of her father, Samuel Greig. With the precocious Mary now someone else's problem, her family started to rest easy again. About how Greig managed not much is known, but he died when Mary was only 33, leaving her a very wealthy widow. No lavish balls and fancy dress parties for the young widow, though; she had much better uses for the money. In no time at all, she had purchased enough books to build a wonderful mathematics library.

Marrying a second time, and by her own choice, she had better luck. William Somerville was an army doctor and a scholar; he also respected his wife's intelligence and encouraged her mathematical and scientific pursuits.

In 1816, when William was transferred to London, Mary suddenly found herself in the center of English scientific life, and she knew what she was going to do. She would write about science. She published *The Connection of the Physical Sciences* in 1834. Her *Physical Geography* (1848) quickly won many scientific admirers, although it was attacked by some of the clergy who were still fighting the old battle against an ancient age for Earth. In fact the book did so well that an organization called The

vatory, complete with telescope, located on a hill in London. He fitted a spectroscope to his telescope and studied the spectral lines emitted by two stars so bright they can be easily seen with the

Society for the Diffusion of Useful Knowledge asked her to write a book on astronomy for them. It, too, won admirers, and she followed with a book on Newton's *Principia*. During the 1820s a woman could not become a professor, but Mary Somerville quickly became a favorite writer of scientists and professors. With the growing specialization of science, it was becoming difficult for the curious scientist to know what was going on in other fields. Drawn by the care and precision of her writing, her brilliant understanding of the facts, and her lucid explanations, more than a few scientists turned to Mary Somerville. John Herschel, excited by her manuscript *Mechanics of the Heavens* (1831), became a good friend and ardent supporter, recommending not only that book but others of hers to his friends. Soon not just scientists were reading Mary Somerville but also the literate public who wanted clear, factual, and readable reports on the growing scientific explosion around them. A science writer of the highest intelligence and wit, Mary Somerville soon found a place at the heart of London's scientific society as the Somerville home became a gathering place for some of the finest minds of her time. Unable to attend a university, Mary Somerville now had a good part of the university attending her gatherings—to the mutual delight and benefit of all.

When the Royal Society of London elected Mary Fairfax Greig Somerville and Caroline Herschel (1750–1848) to membership in 1835, they became the first two women to be so honored for their scientific accomplishments. *(Bettmann/CORBIS)*

naked eye: Aldebaran and Betelgeuse. He could identify the thumbprint of the elements iron, sodium, calcium, magnesium, and bismuth. Next he tried a nebula and, with a feeling of great suspense and awe, stepped up to look. "Was I not about to look into a secret place of creation?" he wrote in his journal. Perhaps this moment would settle once and for all the question of which theory about nebulae was correct.

> I looked into the spectroscope. No spectrum such as I expected! A single bright line only! . . . The riddle of the nebula was solved. The answer, which had come to us in the light itself, read: Not an aggregation of stars, but a luminous gas. Stars after the order of our own sun, and of the brighter stars, would give a different spectrum; the light of this nebula had clearly been emitted by a luminous gas.

Huggins unfortunately got off on the wrong foot by assuming that, because this nebula was gaseous, all nebulae—including those with elliptical and spiral shapes—were made of gas. But, nonetheless, the first use of spectroscopy in astronomy was a stunning success. Fraunhofer's lines and the spectroscope functioned for astronomical research in much the same role as fossils do in geology, providing invaluable information on temperatures, compositions, and motions of gaseous nebulae and stars. As Kirchhoff showed, a hot, glowing, opaque object emits a continuous spectrum—a complete rainbow of colors without spectral lines. Viewed through a cool gas, though, dark spectral absorption lines appear in the spectrum. These reveal the chemical makeup of the gas. If, however, the gas is viewed at an angle, a different set of patterns appear. These tools have become a sort of Rosetta stone for astronomers studying the gaseous nebulae.

Photographing the Stars

John Herschel (1792–1871), son of William Herschel, was one of the first to recognize the possibilities photography had for astronomy. (In fact John Herschel coined the word *photography*.) Although photography was discovered in 1826, it was not initially used for astronomy until the 1840s. Once the tool was introduced, it caught on and, though now coupled with computers, photography remains a key tool for astronomy. Its great advantage was, of course, that working from photographic plates, astronomers no longer had to work in real time. They could pore over the plates for hours anytime after the photographic image was captured. They could focus on specific areas using a magnifying glass or a telescope, and they could compare plates taken at different times. They also had more accurate records than anyone could draw by hand, no matter how sharp one's eyesight might be. As the medium of photography became more versatile, it became possible to leave a plate exposed for periods of time to catch objects that could not otherwise be seen, even with a telescope. In 1889 Edward Emerson Barnard photographed the Milky Way for the first time. Photography would become more and more important as a tool for astronomers in years to come, and today vast databases of images exist for research and study.

John Herschel, son of Caroline's brother William Herschel, undertook the immense task of extending his father's catalog of stars to the Southern Hemisphere. He was also a pioneer in the use of photography in astronomy and in measurements of solar energy output. (© *UC Regents; Lick Observatory image, Mary Lea Shane Archives of Lick Observatory*)

Second-Guessing the Sun

The closest star, of course, and the most important to us is our own Sun, and the 19th century saw two discoveries that added to the understanding of solar physics. In 1843 Samuel Heinrich Schwabe announced his discovery of the cyclic action of sunspots. Galileo had been the first to detect the presence of spots on the Sun, and now Schwabe's recognition of their cycle gave a new view into the inner workings of the Sun. The discovery marked the beginning of early work in solar physics and astrophysics. Another surprise was the discovery of an element in the Sun's composition that had never been detected on Earth. Discovered by Pierre-Jules-César Janssen in 1868, the existence of helium first came to light during the study of the Sun's spectral lines.

Meanwhile Lord Kelvin and Helmholtz both thought the age of the Earth was 20 to 22 million years at most, based on their ideas of the interior heat mechanisms of the Sun. But geologists and biologists of the day were coming up with vastly different figures for Earth's age. In an ongoing search for a definitive age for Earth, Lord Kelvin investigated geomagnetism, hydrodynamics, the shape of the Earth, and the geophysical determination of the Earth's age. He soon found himself at the center of a controversy concerning the age of the Earth because his estimated age of the Sun at only 20 million years was not nearly long enough for a gradual process of biologic evolution to take place on Earth, whereas geologists such as James Hutton and Charles Lyell postulated a much longer span of history for the Earth. Darwin, in formulating his evolutionary theory (see chapter 6), was using Lyell's figures that Earth's geological history spanned at least 300 million years. More recent, 21st-century understanding of the heat mechanisms of the Sun supports Darwin rather than Kelvin.

Gauging Earth's Age

Earth scientists were an entirely different breed from astronomers. Although miners and engineers had long made a study of the ground we walk on, unlike astronomy, geology as a science did not begin to develop until the 18th century and did not reach full bloom until the 19th century.

The 1700s had closed with a great controversy raging among geologists, every investigator lining up with one faction or the other—either the neptunists or the plutonists. The captain of the neptunists was Abraham Gottlob Werner (1750–1817), a prominent German geologist who maintained that all Earth's layers were laid down as sediment by the waters of a primeval flood. Chief of the plutonists was a Scottish geologist, James Hutton (1726–97), who contended that the chief driving mechanism in the Earth's formation was heat within, which periodically broke through the crust in the form of volcanoes.

Of the two schools the plutonists were the more radical. The neptunists saw the Earth's history as a once-and-for-all occurrence, a giant flood (similar to the biblical story of Noah) that laid down the Earth's crust in its current form. This fit best with a literal interpretation of the biblical story of creation—from which scholars concluded that Earth could be no more than about 6,000 years old. Hutton and the plutonists, on the other hand, maintained that

Earth's history had seen a long, slow, continuing process of change over greatly extended periods of time. They thought that the same forces now observed working on Earth's surface had always been at work. The forming, wearing down, and reforming processes had repeated over and over again. Other processes had also been going on continually for eons—such as molten lava from within, pushing up through Earth's crust; the formation of new, crystalline rocks such as basalt and granite; and the tilting of sedimentary layers of rock at the surface. This point of view was considered radical and rationalist (a point of view accepting reason as the only authority) and received much skepticism at the outset.

The great French comparative anatomist Georges Cuvier (Baron Cuvier) (1769–1832) numbered among those who objected. Cuvier saw evidence of a series of catastrophes in Earth's history, during which all species were wiped out and after which new rock strata were laid down. The most recent of these catastrophes, he said, was the flood described in the biblical tradition.

Swiss-American geologist Louis Agassiz (1807–73) held an independent catastrophe theory that Earth had suffered an ice age—as many as 20 of them, in fact—counting as evidence some of the current movements and behavior of glaciers and glacial evidence in areas where no glaciers now exist. Although the ice age theory was rejected at first, it gradually became accepted as evidence piled up.

Often called the Heroic Age of Geology, the period from 1790 to 1830 was a time when geology experienced considerable influence from the Romantic movement in arts and philosophy. The Romantics embraced Nature (with a capital *N*) and encouraged exploration of exotic lands. Romantics gladly turned their backs on polite, stifling society to explore the wilds of uncultured Nature, untamed and unspoiled by human touch. Travel to scenically dramatic locales became popular, and for the scientists who answered the call of this yearning, fieldwork in a wide variety of terrain put them face to face with formations and strata they might otherwise never have encountered. Whereas much of geology, up to this time, had been the study of mineralogy and identification of isolated rock specimens, it now had become a visionary science that read strata for their saga of revolutions, decay, and restoration—an epic tale of great, warring Earth forces.

The old guard, of course, persisted. These were the geologists who continued the practical surveying tradition of the past and who concerned themselves with the professional standing of their science, the collection of evidence, and the sound formulation of theory. The Romantic group, often in conflict with more traditional geologists, saw themselves as knights in the pursuit of Truth, prepared to face its radical consequences and committed to the exploration of Nature.

These two mindsets did not necessarily divide along ideological lines, however, or substantially affect the methods used. The conservative, religious, and anti-Revolutionary frame of mind that characterized the years following the French Revolution enforced on geology a strict adherence to empiricism—that is, the support of theory with meticulous evidence. The result was that even those influenced by freewheeling Romanticism examined strata and collected specimens in much the same way as their colleagues.

By 1830 a much larger body of facts existed from which to draw theory, and the cause of Hutton's uniformitarianism had attracted a wealthy young Scottish lawyer who was more drawn to geology than to law. Though he studied geology at Oxford under a neptunist, Charles Lyell traveled widely in Europe and had the opportunity to examine many strata of rock for himself. From his studies he came to the conclusion that Hutton was right, that the forces that had fashioned the history of the Earth were uniform over time and were the same as those still effecting erosion and sedimentation, heating and cooling in the modern era. He was also widely read—more so

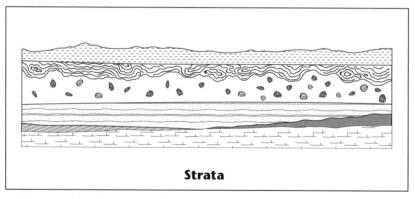

Strata

Geologists in the 19th century studied strata like these, observed by geologist Charles Lyell in the Norfolk cliffs of England, to determine the history of the Earth. (The Geological Evidences of the Antiquity of Man, *by Sir Charles Lyell, 1863)*

Sideroads of Science: The Hollow-Earth Theory

As divergent as the opinions of Lyell, Hutton, and Cuvier were, some people in the 19th century had a much more bizarre opinion: that the Earth was hollow and the interior was accessible by openings at both poles. Arguably a crackpot notion, the idea had a pedigreed history. British astronomer Edmond Halley proposed in the late 17th century that Earth's interior was composed of concentric spheres—four of them to be exact—and he also speculated that the interior space was populated and filled with a glowing atmosphere. Holes at the poles allowed light to escape into the atmosphere we breathe on the surface, and that is why, he explained, we see the *aurora borealis* near the North Pole.

The theory gained new life in the early 19th century from John Symmes, a veteran of the War of 1812. Thanks to his popularization of Halley's vision, the supposed hole at the pole was named Symmes Hole. Symmes tried to gather interest in an expedition to the North Pole to investigate the opening to the inner world but died unsatisfied in 1829.

In 1869 an alchemist and herbalist named Cyrus Reed Teed reported having a vision that instructed him that we actually are living inside the Earth, not on its surface as we thought. He made speeches, handed out pamphlets, and even founded a cult based on his vision.

The hollow Earth theme has turned up in numerous works of fiction, including Edgar Allan Poe's *The Narrative of Arthur Gordon Pym of Nantucket* (1838) and Jules Verne's *Journey to the Center of the Earth* (1864).

This myth has continued into the 21th century, with UFOs using the poles as portals for traveling in and out of the globe. The interior civilization is said to be more advanced than ours, both spiritually and technologically. This despite the fact that many pilots have flown their airplanes over the poles and satellites beam images from space showing—no holes! It is unquestionably a good science fiction story, though.

than Hutton—and though he made no discovery, nor fashioned any theory himself, his great gift was that he brought many facts together in one work.

Charles Lyell founded the theory of uniformitarianism in geology. *(Courtesy of the National Library of Medicine)*

Only the geological forces now in effect should be considered as explanations for past history, he maintained, and very long periods of time should be assumed. He wrote: "Confined notions in regard to the quantity of past time have tended more than any other pre-possessions to retard the progress of geology and until we habituate ourselves to contemplate the possibility of an indefinite lapse of ages . . . we shall be in danger of forming most erroneous views in geology."

In 1830 Lyell published the first volume of *The Principles of Geology: Being an Attempt to Explain the Former Changes of the Earth's Surface by Reference to Causes Now in Operation.* One copy was destined to become well thumbed as it began a journey the following year aboard the HMS *Beagle,* the most famous voyage in the history of science. The book's owner was Charles Darwin.

PART II

The Life Sciences
in the Nineteenth Century

6

Darwin and the *Beagle*'s Bounty

EVOLUTION, AS AN IDEA, WAS IN the air at the beginning of the 19th century. Geologists were debating the issue of the evolution of the Earth. The discussion naturally went hand-in-hand with the question of biological evolution. Fossils raised questions. Vestigial organs tweaked the imagination. But it was an explosive issue. For this era it was almost as dangerous to put forth as Copernicanism had been in Galileo's day. Certainly ideas about evolution were bound to cause a furor.

Lyell himself was drawn to the idea, but he preferred, at least at first, to let it alone. In 1836 he wrote to the astronomer John Herschel:

> In regards to the origination of new species, I am very glad to find
> that you think it probable that it may be carried on through the
> intervention of intermediate causes. I left this rather to be inferred,
> not thinking it worth while to offend a certain class of persons by
> embodying in words what would only be a speculation.

The volatility of the subject was not lost on Charles Darwin (1809–82), who, in any case, set out at the beginning of his career with no aim to prove any such point.

Voyage of the *Beagle*

Initially Charles Darwin had not planned to be a biologist. His grandfather, Erasmus Darwin, had been a biologist of sorts and had even offered a theory of evolution, but professionally he was a physician.

(Charles's other grandfather, Josiah Wedgwood, was a porcelain manufacturer with an interest in chemistry. Both grandfathers had been core members of a scientific philosophical society known as the Lunar Society.) Charles's father was also a physician, and Charles initially planned to follow the family tradition but quickly discovered he had no stomach for it. He planned instead to train for the clergy, but at Cambridge University his love for rambling alone outdoors found a suitable outlet in botanical field trips. He also became friends with his botany professor, John Stevens Henslow, to whose home he was often invited for dinner and conversation. "His knowledge," Darwin later wrote, "was great in botany, entomology, chemistry, mineralogy, and geology. His strongest taste was to draw conclusions from long-continued minute observations." During their long talks Darwin soaked up both content and method. Henslow was impressed with the enthusiasm and ability of his young student, and, hearing of an opportunity for a naturalist to sail under Captain Robert FitzRoy on the HMS *Beagle*, he did not hesitate to recommend young Darwin.

The *Beagle*'s mission, commissioned by the British Admiralty, was a five-year voyage to map the coasts of Patagonia, Tierra del Fuego, Chile, and Peru; to fix longitude; and to establish a chain of chronological calculations around the world. It was customary to take a nat-

The HMS *Beagle* at the Straits of Magellan at the southern tip of South America (*Stock Montage, Inc.*)

uralist along on voyages of this kind, if for no other reason than to provide intelligent and gentlemanly company for the ship's captain.

The *Beagle* set sail on December 27, 1831. The accommodations were cramped—a shared cabin with the captain, a moody man at best—and there was scant room for the equipment Darwin needed for his work. In the tiny, mahogany-lined compartment, he slept in a hammock that swung mercilessly with every pitch of the ship, and he was plagued with seasickness throughout the voyage. "The absolute want of room is an evil," he wrote dismally in his journal at the outset, "that nothing can surmount."

With him Darwin took four books: the Bible, a copy of Milton, Alexander von Humboldt's account of his exploration of Venezuela and the Orinocco basin, and—unquestionably most important to his scientific future—volume one of Lyell's *Principles of Geology*. On arrival in Montevideo on the eastern shore of the South American continent, Darwin found volume two waiting for him, thoughtfully sent by Henslow, to whom the *Beagle's* naturalist kept up a continual flow of reports (many of them read by Henslow at meetings of the Philosophical Society of Cambridge). Volume three awaited the *Beagle's* docking at Valparaiso, on the other side of the continent.

On the high seas the voyage may have been a nightmare, but the shoreside opportunities for exploration and observation were a naturalist's paradise. On land Darwin was in his element. With clear, evocative prose, he rose to the occasion in his journals (which were published in five volumes in the 10 years following his return). Off the shore of Tenerife, he wrote:

> . . . the air is still & deliciously warm—the only sounds are the waves rippling on the stern & the sails idly flapping round the masts . . . The sky is so clear & lofty, & stars innumerable shine so bright that like little moons they cast their glitter on the waves.

On landing, while FitzRoy set up his observatory to take the measurements the Admiralty had sent him to make, Darwin hiked inland or explored the coast, accompanied by interpreters and, sometimes, other ships' officers. He was impressed by the primeval force of nature, lush undergrowth, exotic birds, and animals, and, on the coast, brightly colored sponges and intricate tropical corals. South America held a vast store of plants and animals that Darwin had never seen before: wild llamas in Patagonia, giant tortoises in the Galápagos Islands, pansy orchids in Brazil, fossil seashells high in the Andes, corals in the Indian Ocean. He sent hundreds of specimens home to Henslow and made copious notes and drawings.

In the Galápagos he was struck in particular by a series of finches (now known as "Darwin's finches") living on widely spaced isles that varied in many ways from those found on the mainland. Similar in size and color, 13 different species had developed with different beak shapes, each adapted, apparently, to its unique feeding niche. A seed-eater had a beak that worked well for cracking seed hulls. Another, on a different island where seeds were not available, had a long, sharp beak that worked well for eating its diet of insects. Another, a vegetarian finch, had a short, fat beak that could pluck the buds and leaves it fed on, and so on. Darwin was deeply impressed, he wrote later in his *Autobiography,* by the manner in which the species in the Galápagos "differ slightly on each island of the group, none of these islands appearing to be very ancient in a geological sense. It was evident that such factors as these, as well as many others, could be explained on the supposition that species gradually became modified; and the subject haunted me."

The second volume of *The Principles of Geology* by Lyell had already begun to raise some of these issues. Lyell had made a study of the geographic distribution of plants and animals, and he had formed the theory that each species had come into being in one center. "Similar habitats on separate continents," he wrote, "seemed to produce quite different species" that were well equipped to survive in their particular habitats. Here Lyell applied his uniformitarian concepts to biology. New species had constantly emerged, he said, throughout the history of the Earth; others had become extinct along the way. Since geologic processes were constantly in a state of flux, as they were still, the inception and extinction of species constantly took place in response. A highly successful species might crowd out others in competition for food in the same habitat, resulting in extinction of some species. But Lyell stopped short of "transmutation" of species. A new species might come into existence, but it would not change, or evolve, over time.

Pre-Darwinian Evolution

Biology had reached this point by stages. In 1686 John Ray had defined the modern concept of species, based on descent from a common ancestral type, and the comte de Buffon (Georges-Louis Leclerc) clarified this in 1749: A species is a group of interbreeding individuals who cannot breed successfully outside the group. But these early biologists assumed that the species had not changed since the beginning of time. Hampered by their assumptions, they were locked into a concept known as the Great Chain of Being, with all species part of an unbroken chain from the lowliest creature at the bottom to humans and angels at the pinnacle. All species were fixed, having the same characteristics they had always had since the beginning of time. In the 17th and 18th centuries, most scientists had subscribed to an idea called preformation that assumed that every adult was already preformed either in the egg or in the sperm (depending which of two warring factions on this point they subscribed to). This theory was a roadblock to development of the theory of evolution, but it was soon replaced by the theory of epigenesis, established by Casper Wolff, who saw that an embryo develops not from a tiny preformed creature but from undifferentiated tissues. The emergence of the theory of epigenesis was the first major step necessary to open the door to an evolutionary theory of the origin of species.

The second factor to prepare the way toward the end of the 18th century and the beginning of the 19th was the understanding of fossils and the fact that they represented the bones of species that no longer existed (see sidebar on page 88).

The third precondition to emerge was the growing recognition, also toward the end of the 18th century and the beginning of the 19th, that the Earth was very, very old. In fact, James Hutton and Charles Lyell maintained that the formations present in the Earth's crust could only have been produced over great stretches of time. These stretches of time were sufficiently vast (Lyell estimated 240 million years) that evolutionary changes in species might not be observable in living species. (This is in fact the case: We generally cannot observe evolutionary changes at the species level within a lifetime.)

So, by the beginning of the 19th century, many scientists had begun to entertain ideas of some form of evolution. Jean-Baptiste de Monet, chevalier de Lamarck, who was one of the first evolutionists, correctly proposed that species evolve in response to the environment. He also thought, however, that acquired characteristics could be inherited by offspring, an idea with which most scientists of his day and since have disagreed. For instance, a giraffe, he said, could

Cope and Marsh:
Rival Bone Hunters

Dinosaur fossils—huge fragments of fossilized bone from the skulls and skeletons of creatures that died millions of years ago—offered one of the most dramatic types of evidence for Darwin's contentions that the Earth was very old and that species had changed over time. During the mid-1800s the American West and Midwest proved to be a bone hunter's paradise for paleontologists seeking dinosaur bones. Two of the most successful and most respected of the American bone hunters were Edward Drinker Cope (1840–97) and Othniel C. Marsh (1831–99). Scouring through the West with ferocious intensity, the two men collected an astounding array of dinosaur finds, published hundreds of papers, and enriched the collections of many museums. None of this was done in a cooperative spirit, however. The two men hated each other, and it was often said that they mounted their western expeditions more like raiding parties than carefully planned scientific expeditions.

Neither could be considered "innocent" in the conflict. Cope was wealthy, egotistical, belligerent, and often—as Marsh shouted accusingly—dishonest. Marsh was wealthy, egotistical, belligerent, and often—as Cope shouted accusingly—dishonest! Many of their contemporaries were happy that the two men hated each other so much and spent so much time trying to best the other: The fact that they focused their unpleasant personalities and unscrupulous activities on each other kept them pretty much out of everybody else's hair.

At least some of the time. Once, when he was visiting Cape Cod, Cope watched from a distance while a team of scientists from Harvard University worked all day to cut away the decaying flesh of a gigantic whale that had washed ashore. The huge skeleton was being prepared to be sent to the Agassiz Museum at Harvard. After the team had finished their work, loaded the bones on a railroad flatcar, and wearily left for home and rest, Cope came out of hiding and bribed the railway stationmaster to switch the destination on the shipment card from the Harvard museum to his own museum in Philadelphia, Pennsylvania. It was a few years before the Harvard team discovered how their gigantic skeleton had become lost.

A group of bone searchers sponsored by Othniel Marsh. In the 1880s Marsh and Edward Cope raced each other to see which of them could dig up the greater collection of fossil bones from the midwestern and western United States. *(Yale University Archives)*

Most of Cope's raiding, though, took place at Marsh's expense, and Marsh paid him back in kind. Typical of their behavior toward one another was the time when Cope made a deal with an amateur bone hunter for some important bones Cope wanted. Cope promised the man he would send him a check and collect the bones—and then proceeded to write a paper on them. Marsh, though, also heard about the amateur's find and sent a message to the man, pretending to be a Cope associate and canceling the deal. Then Marsh bought the specimens himself.

The rivalry became so absurd at times that it threw American paleontology into confusion. Not the most careful of scholars, both rushed into print often, and since they often covered the same territory, they often found the same species at the same time, which they both then went about naming—resulting in many dinosaurs with two different names and leaving the mess of sorting the whole thing out to later paleontologists.

Although they conducted much of their science in a decidedly ungentlemanly and an often unscientific manner (Cope often dynamited his research sites after he was finished with them so no one else could come along and get to something he might have missed!), the two buccaneering paleontologists together discovered and named more than 1,718 new genera and species of fossil animals from the American West.

make its neck longer by stretching toward the leaves high in the trees and could pass this acquired trait on to its offspring.

The Origin of Species

On his return from the voyage of the *Beagle* in 1836, Darwin was troubled by his observations, and yet he was not prepared to draw conclusions about the evolution of species. Finally, in May 1837, he began a notebook on evidence for transmutation. Then in 1838 he came across *An Essay on the Principle of Population,* a book published in 1798 by English economist Thomas Robert Malthus (1766–1834). Not about biology at all, Malthus's essay proposed that human populations increase geometrically (e.g., 2, 4, 8, 16 . . .), while means to support them increase only arithmetically (e.g., 1, 2, 3, 4, 5 . . .). So, he said, natural selective forces—such as overcrowding, disease, war, poverty, and vice—take over to weed out those that are less fit. Those that are fittest survive.

In his notebooks Darwin had used the words *descent* and *modification.* Now, thanks to Malthus, he had a new term to describe the process for which he had seen evidence: *selection.* He now wrote: "One may say there is a force like a hundred wedges trying [to] force every kind of adapted structure into the gaps in the economy of nature, or rather forming gaps by thrusting out weaker ones."

Ultimately Darwin developed the idea of natural selection in species, a concept that is often referred to as "survival of the fittest." That is, those individuals of a species that are fittest to reproduce are the ones who successfully pass on their traits to later generations (even though these "fittest" may not necessarily be the strongest or the best). For Darwin the idea was beginning to gel. In the true tradition of Francis Bacon, he had set out with no preconceived ideas about what he would find, had collected voluminous evidence, and now had spent time reflecting on it and analyzing it. In 1842 he began to write a 1,500-word synopsis. By July 1844 he had written a 15,000-word essay, which he showed to his friend botanist Joseph Dalton Hooker (1817–1911).

That same year Robert Chambers published a book called *Vestiges of the Natural History of Creation* that set forth a theory of evolution, which intrigued Darwin. Although Chambers's book had popular appeal, however, Chambers offered no explanation for evo-

Charles Darwin at the age of 40, at the time he was working on barnacles *(Courtesy of the National Library of Medicine)*

lution and was not careful, making many errors that discredited him with most scientists.

Determined to make certain that his own work was so thorough and well documented it would be irreproachable, Darwin embarked on an eight-year study of fossil and living forms of barnacles. He examined 10,000 specimens, publishing four monographs on his work between the years 1851 and 1854. It was exhausting, meticulous work, and tedious, but, at the end of it, Darwin felt he had the right to call himself not just the collector and observer he had been aboard the *Beagle* but now also a truly trained naturalist.

During this period he came upon a key idea, the idea of divergence. How did differences between varieties become so pronounced that they became differences that separate species—differences that made inter-breeding impossible? "The more diversified the descendants from any one species became in structure, constitution and habits," he wrote, "by so much will they be better enabled to seize on many and widely diversified places" in nature's structure. That very diversification, that branching off, took them further and further from the original stock.

By now he had become good friends with Lyell, who at first rejected Darwin's ideas about evolution. Now Lyell, Hooker, and Darwin's brother Erasmus all encouraged him to begin writing a book that would set out his theory definitively and provide all the documentation he could amass to support it. Darwin began writing. "I am working very hard at my book," he wrote to a cousin in February 1858, "perhaps too hard. It will be very big; and I have become most deeply interested in the way facts fall into groups . . . I mean to make my book as perfect as I can. I shall not go to press at soonest for a couple of years."

Letter from Malaysia

But Darwin's "big book" would never be completed. With 250,000 words written, on June 18, 1858, he received an astounding letter from a fellow naturalist working in Malaysia. Would Darwin read the enclosed essay and, if he thought it worthy, pass it on? The essay, which treated "the tendency of varieties to depart indefinitely from the original type," by Alfred Russel Wallace (1823–1913), delineated the same theory of evolution Charles Darwin had been working on for 20 years! The resemblance was uncanny.

Completely dismayed, Darwin sought the advice of Lyell and Hooker, who suggested he explain the predicament to Wallace and propose a common announcement of the theory, taking joint priority. Darwin followed the suggestion and was delighted to hear from Wallace that he was most happy to make a joint announcement. Actually the younger man had spent much less time and much less care developing the theory, and he profited from Darwin's stature. So in 1858 Wallace's essay appeared in the *Journal of the Linnean Society* along with a summary by Darwin of his work.

Darwin published his shortened version in book form on November 22, 1859: *On the Origin of Species by Means of Natural Selection, or the Preservation of Favoured Races in the Struggle for Life* (usually known just as *On the Origin of Species* or the *Origin of Species*). Every copy of the original 1,250-copy printing was sold on the first day. Even in this shortened form, it is a very long and persuasive argument for evolution, supported by many, many examples, and it succeeded in convincing a substantial number of biologists of its truth.

Based on his own observations, Alfred Russel Wallace independently came up with many of the same ideas about evolution as Darwin. *(Courtesy of the National Library of Medicine)*

Descent of Man

But, while most scientists accepted Darwin and Wallace's evolutionary theory and the idea of natural selection, the public was slower to go along with these ideas. Many considered Darwinism to be atheistic—and, in fact, Darwin had struggled long and hard with this issue himself. If organisms adapted through the mechanistic process of natural selection, where was the role of God in the creation or continuing development of the world and its creatures?

Some scientists also balked mightily. Richard Owens, a renowned geologist at Oxford University in England, and Louis Agassiz at Harvard University in the United States were numbered among the most vocal scientific opponents. Agassiz, a highly reputed, knowledgeable naturalist with a gift for popularization, maintained that organisms on Earth had been formed during a series of creations by a Supreme Being. According to this view organisms became more complex and better adapted to their surroundings over time as a result of the successive stages of a supernatural creation.

Adam Sedgwick, an old-school geologist from Cambridge University, was another opponent of Darwin's theory, remarking in 1865 of his colleague Charles Lyell:

> Lyell has swallowed the whole theory [of evolution], at which I am not surprised, for without it the elements of geology as he expounded them were illogical. . . . They may varnish it as they will, but the transmutation theory ends, with nine out of ten, in rank materialism.

A talented naturalist, Louis Agassiz introduced the idea that Earth was once covered with glaciers (*Studies on Glaciers,* 1840) and completed an extensive study of fish fossils (*Researches on Fossil Fishes,* 1833–44). However, instead of Darwin's natural selection, Agassiz proposed a periodic intervention by the Creator in an attempt to explain the apparent changes and evolution in plant and animal species. (*Edgar Fahs Smith Collection—University of Pennsylvania Library*)

If one species evolved from another, the most troubling point for most people, though, was the idea—assiduously avoided by Darwin in his book—that human beings must have descended from a nonhuman ancestor.

The controversy became hotter and hotter. Apelike cartoons of Darwin appeared in newspapers. Essays and sermons proliferated everywhere. Darwin had never recovered from the untimely death of his daughter Annie and was in ill health, which only became worse as the controversy raged. He was, in any case, of no temperament to combat the furor. That is where T. H. Huxley came in. Huxley (1825–95), who had read *On the Origin of Species* with relish ("Why didn't I think of that?" he wanted to know), leaped to the lecture platform in Darwin's place. Calling himself "Darwin's bulldog" (Huxley always loved a good intellectual fight), he debated the issue of evolution with zeal wherever and whenever he could.

Before a packed audience of 700, Huxley met the Bishop of Oxford, Samuel Wilberforce (known as "Soapy Sam," for his slippery manner and unctuous speech), in a grand debate for the British Association for the Advancement of Science. But Wilberforce, probably primed by Owens with "facts," lost the day before the Victorian audience when he snidely inquired which of Huxley's parents descended from the apes, his father or his mother.

Darwin in his 60s, about 15 years after publication of *On the Origin of Species* *(Courtesy of the National Library of Medicine)*

Huxley knew when he had an edge and he used it. The audience was there for a show, and the quick-witted Huxley provided it. Better to be descended from an ape, he replied evenly, than from an educated man who would introduce such a question into a serious scientific debate. For that, Wilberforce had no retort.

In 1863 Lyell finally took up the cause with a book entitled *Geological Evidence of the Antiquity of Man.* He came out in favor of Darwinism, though a bit more timidly than his friend would have liked. He did indicate that humans or humanlike creatures must have existed for many millennia on the face of the Earth. But he did not say openly that he believed in transmutation or that humans had evolved from apelike creatures.

In 1871 Darwin came out with *The Descent of Man, and Selection in Relation to Sex,* in which he supported the idea that humans descended from pre-human creatures, supported by considerable evidence from his research. Humans possess vestigial points on their ears, he pointed out, and muscles that obviously were once used to move the

Because of Huxley's defense of Darwin's *Origin of the Species* and natural selection, his name, like Darwin's, became a household commonplace, with references and caricatures—such as this one from *Vanity Fair*—appearing in magazines and newspapers all over the world. *(Courtesy of the National Library of Medicine)*

ears. The "tail-bone," or coccyx, at the base of the spine he cited as another example of a now-useless appendage that appeared to be left over from an earlier phase in the history of the species *Homo sapiens.*

Resistance to these ideas continued in some sectors—George Bernard Shaw also opposed Darwinism, subscribing instead to Lamarckianism and a kind of mystical life force. As late as 1936, H. G. Wells wrote *The Croquet Player,* which examined the unease of the civilized English gentry when faced with the knowledge of the "brute within." But most people were won over by the end of the 19th century, except for those who opposed evolution as antithetical to the biblical story of creation.

More Proof

There were still some problems, though. Would a variation in one individual, however successful, not become blended into intermediate, less successful versions as a new trait was passed on to the offspring of later generations? How could natural selection ever have the opportunity to operate on successful variations?

A lone Augustinian monk from Austria named Gregor Mendel, running experiments with dwarf and tall strains of peas in the monastery garden, came up with the proof in the 1850s and 1860s. Mendel discovered that for each trait, an offspring apparently inherited factors from *both* parents equally. Most important he found that those factors are not blended but remain distinct and can, in turn, be passed on, unblended, to subsequent offspring. This meant that natural selection would have much more time to operate on any variation in a trait. Unfortunately Mendel's work did not become widely known until it was rediscovered at the beginning of the 20th century.

Evolutionary theory has not stopped growing; many

T. H. Huxley, defender of the theory of evolution and Darwin's ideas about natural selection *(Courtesy of the National Library of Medicine)*

The Neandertal Mystery

When workers unearthed a partial humanlike skull and skeleton from a limestone cave near the village of Neander, Germany, in 1856, they also unearthed a mystery that continues today.

The renowned French paleontologist Georges Cuvier (1769–1832) had argued hotly that no fossils of ancient humans would ever be discovered for the simple reason that they did not exist. Cuvier was what we would call today an anti-evolutionist, and most of the scientific world before Darwin agreed with him.

To whom did those strange bones belong, then—and strange they were, with a heavy skullcap and nearly a dozen and a half curiously "deformed" skeletal parts. The most obvious guess that came to the first German professors who examined the bones was that they were definitely not German, but probably belonged to some much wilder and older northern tribe. Rudolf Carl Virchow [FEER-koh], Germany's most respected anatomist, did not believe they were even ancient but thought they most likely belonged to an unfortunate cripple with a badly deformed skull who also suffered from arthritis. Another German anatomist, perhaps wondering about the consequences of such a strange-looking individual wandering around the German countryside, suggested that such a person might even have been mentally "abnormal" and lived as a hermit in the cave in which the bones had been found.

Today, after Darwin, and now that more and more of the so-called Neandertal skeletons have been found in places ranging as far apart as North Africa, France, Israel, and China, we know that the Neandertals, like many other human-fossil finds, do have a place in the story of human evolution. But exactly what place still is not certain.

Early portraits of Neandertals, based primarily on that first find in the Neander Valley, portrayed a stooped, hulking, shambling creature with brutish intelligence—the "ape man" of countless bad movies. For many in the 19th century and well into the 20th, this portrayal of Neandertals as the direct ancestor of *Homo sapiens* raised deeply troubling questions about "the beast within" us all. Ironically some of the earliest guesses about the first Neander Valley specimen's serious arthritic deformity, if not about its age, have turned out to be correct. More recent finds have indicated a much less stooped stature and appearance.

Neandertals roamed the world beginning about 130,000 years ago and disappeared about 35,000 years ago. They were short and squat; the

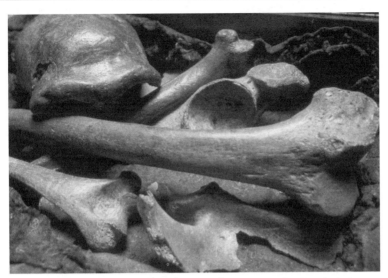

The first Neandertal was discovered in Neander, Germany in 1856, just as Darwin's ideas were causing many people to reexamine their ideas about human origins. Compared to a modern human skull, the Neandertal had a heavy brow ridge, sloping forehead, and thick walls. The modern human skull has a flatter face and thinner walls. *(John Reader/Science Photo Library/Photo Researchers, Inc.)*

men probably averaged only a little over five feet, and the women were slightly shorter. They walked erect, made tools, and lived in social groups. Ceremonial objects occasionally found with the dead also suggest that they may have developed a fairly advanced religious system.

But the long-standing mystery remains: What relationship did Neandertals have with modern humans, and why did they disappear from the face of the Earth? Through the end of the Victorian era, most scientists believed that Neandertals were our direct ancestors, but more recent findings in the 20th century show that our direct ancestors—the Cro-Magnons—lived at the same time as the Neandertals. As a result some serious questions have cropped up about the Neandertal's direct relationship to us.

Perhaps the biggest mystery, though, about these intriguing people is what happened to them to have caused their complete disappearance about 35,000 years ago. Did our direct ancestors, the Cro-Magnon,

(continues)

(continued)

systematically and violently kill off their Neandertal neighbors, as some have suggested? Did Cro-Magnon and Neandertal mix and inter-breed, gradually merging into one population, as others argue? Recent DNA studies reported in 2003 show that this is not likely, although they do show that humans and Neandertals had a common ancestor some 500,000 years ago. Did they, like many other populations before them, simply lose out in the long-term battle for survival, gradually diminishing until extinction finally overcame them? The record shows that they dominated Europe for 100,000 years and were a highly successful species. We still don't know what happened or why they disappeared.

20th- and 21st-century biologists have added to Darwin and Wallace's original theory and have incorporated newer knowledge about the genetic mechanics of mutation and heredity. Emerging theories about the history of the Earth have also contributed to modern evolutionary theory, including the idea that periods of stability on the Earth's surface have been "punctuated" by times of extreme change, most recently proposed by paleontologists Stephen Jay Gould (1941–2002) and Niles Eldredge (1943–   ).

Charles Darwin died of a heart attack at his home on April 19, 1882. His pallbearers included those who had stood by his side in science—Huxley, Wallace, Hooker, and Sir John Lubbock—and he was buried at Westminster Abbey with Sir Isaac Newton and Sir Charles Lyell. Darwin, however, was never knighted by the British monarch and no statue of him joins the other giants of his century in Madame Tussaud's wax museum in London—perhaps as a caution against vandalism. For this quiet, orderly man with a great respect for natural law stirred up mammoth controversies in his time that remain thorny for some people to this day. He has come to symbolize the intellectual doubts of his century—although, of course, he in no way created them single-handedly. Charles Darwin's ideas about evolution were neither new nor complete. But they did spawn a revolution, altering for all time humanity's understanding of itself and its own place in the natural universe.

7

From Macro to Micro

Organs, Germs, and Cells

EVOLUTION LOOMS LIKE A GIANT in the history of 19th-century life science, but it was not the only area of research that saw important new developments. François Magendie and Claude Bernard in France were pioneers in the fields of experimental physiology, pharmacology, and nutrition. Ivan Pavlov in Russia gained important insights about the functioning of the brain. Louis Pasteur, arguably one of the three most important biologists in the history of science, established insights into the mechanisms that make organisms sick. Theodor Schwann and Matthias Schleiden together discovered that for living organisms nature had another basic building block above the level of molecules: the cell.

Experimental Physiology

Science benefits from no single trait more than a strong spirit of inquiry and zest for knowledge. But, while François Magendie (1783–1855) opened up many avenues of research and pioneered in important areas of experimental physiology, his lack of sensitivity about his experimentation raised enormous controversy in his time and would probably raise even more today. Recognizing that often the most complete knowledge came from seeing living tissue as it functioned—especially in the case of experiments on motor nerves— he did most of his experiments on living organisms (usually dogs), which brought the antivivisectionist activists up in arms against him. Described as irascible and ruthless, he depicted his own activity as an "orgy of experimentation." He often experimented when it was not necessary, pushing beyond the limits of decency, and he earned a decidedly negative reputation.

Magendie nonetheless did make scientific progress that solidly expanded knowledge, even though his methods lacked humanity. He demonstrated the functions of the spinal nerves, showing that the anterior nerve roots of the spinal cord are motor (conveying messages to enact movement) and the posterior nerve roots are sensory (conveying messages to the brain regarding sensations). He also investigated the mechanisms of blood flow, as well as swallowing and vomiting. Magendie introduced the use of strychnine, morphine, brucine, codeine, and quinine, as well as the compounds of iodine and bromine, into medical practice. What he may have done best, however, was to pass on his gusto for research to his students and assistants without infecting them with his disregard for his research subjects.

One of these was Claude Bernard (1813–78), who became Magendie's assistant in 1847 and succeeded him as professor in 1855 when his mentor died. An excellent experimentalist, Bernard is considered to be the founder of experimental physiology. Unlike Magendie, Bernard planned his experiments carefully and integrated them, and his contributions to physiology are extensive.

Claude Bernard, founder of experimental physiology (*Courtesy of the National Library of Medicine*)

Bernard studied digestion through fistulas, openings introduced through the wall of the stomach, and he was able to gain considerable insight into the chemical phenomenon of digestion. He was interested in the balance of chemicals in the body—always objectively seeking biochemical explanations when some of his colleagues would tend to invoke vitalism or mysticism—and he discovered the role of the pancreas in the digestion of fat and the glycogenic function of the liver.

Bernard was able to prove that, contrary to prevailing opinion, animal blood contains sugar even when sugar is not present in the diet. He found that animals convert other substances into glucose, or sugar, in the liver; using experimental methods, he was able to track down the presence of glycogen, the chief animal storage carbohydrate, in the liver. He also discovered the synthesis of glycogen, known as glycogenesis, and the breakdown of glycogen into glucose, known as glycogenolysis. (Glycogen is stored in the liver until it is needed for release into the bloodstream to maintain the glucose level.)

Bernard also detected how certain nerves (called vasomotor nerves) control the flow of the blood to the skin, causing capillaries to dilate when the skin needs cooling and causing them to constrict when the body needs to conserve warmth.

In a study of carbon monoxide poisoning, Bernard was the first to provide a physiological explanation of the process by which a drug affects the body. Carbon monoxide, he realized, replaces oxygen molecules in the blood, and the body cannot react quickly enough to prevent death by oxygen starvation.

Unfortunately for Bernard, despite his greater care, his wife abhorred his vivisections and argued with him about his work constantly. She made large contributions to antivivisectionist societies and legally separated from Bernard in 1869. Beset with financial problems, ill health, and family quarrels (his two daughters also campaigned against his work), Bernard once described the life of science as "a superb and dazzlingly lighted hall which may be reached only by passing through a long and ghastly kitchen."

The French Académie des Sciences awarded the grand prize in physiology to Bernard on three different occasions, and he became a senator in 1869. He was the first scientist to whom France gave a public funeral.

Pavlov and the Brain

For early philosophers, the brain represented the seat of the rational soul, which people possessed and which plants and animals did not. In the Middle Ages scholars thought that imagination, reason, common sense, and memory each resided in one of four chambers, or ventricles, in the brain.

The Renaissance brought new methods of examination, and dissection unmasked many of the mysteries of animal (and human) physiology. Scientists even studied the convolutions on the surface of the brain. But as late as the 17th century, the French philosopher René Descartes [day-KART] still clung to many medieval ideas, even though he tried to apply Newtonian principles of mechanization to physiology. Descartes identified the pineal body at the base of the brain as the seat of the human rational soul, which he said received sensory messages and responded to them by controlling the flow of animal spirits through hollow nerves. In this way the rational soul directed the movement of muscles. This was one of the first primitive explanations of reflex action.

The convoluted surface of the human brain led some anatomists, among them the 17th-century English anatomist Thomas Willis (1621–75), to think that particular functions were seated in various areas of the convolutions. The practice of phrenology developed from this idea and bloomed at the end of the 18th century as "the science of the mind." Phrenologists claimed that they could construct a map of the surface of the brain, locating particular areas that controlled such qualities as acquisitiveness and destructiveness (over the ear), moral qualities such as benevolence and spirituality (near the top of the head), and social or domestic inclinations, such as friendship (near the rear of the brain). Bumps on the surface of the skull were said to correlate with relative development of these various areas of the brain, and phrenologists asserted that they could "read" these bumps and analyze personality and character in this way. Phrenology generally was discredited as a science by the 1840s, although it lingered as a popular pseudoscience well into the 1920s. (See chapter 8.)

However, experiments performed by German physiologists Julius Hitzig [HIT-sikh] (1838–1907) and Gustav Fritsch (1838–1927) were the first to show that different parts of the brain do, indeed, control different functions. Hitzig performed experiments on living dogs, showing that stimulation of a particular region of their brains caused contraction of certain muscles. He also showed that damage of particular portions of the brain caused certain muscles to become weakened or paralyzed.

The Scottish neurologist David Ferrier (1843–1928) also did experiments along these lines, on primates as well as dogs, and succeeded in showing that some regions of the brain (motor regions) controlled movement of the muscles and other organs, while others (sensory regions) received sensations from muscles and other organs.

Like Bernard, Ferrier ran up against opposition from animal rights activists of the day, who accused him of cruelty to animals. But he succeeded in showing in court (1882) that valid justification existed for the experiments, which established crucial knowledge about how the brain functions.

Ivan Pavlov (1849–1936), the Russian physiologist, is best known for his experiments with automatic reflexes and animal behavior.

Pavlov's early work, for which he won the 1904 Nobel Prize in physiology or medicine, investigated the physiology of digestion and the autonomic nervous system. In

Russian physiologist Ivan Pavlov's work on conditioned reflexes had wide influence on physiological psychology and education and training methods. *(Courtesy of the National Library of Medicine)*

a dramatic experiment he surgically bypassed the stomach of a dog so that food eaten by the dog would go down its esophagus but never reach its stomach. Strangely enough the stomach's gastric juices flowed anyway, just as if it had received the food. Pavlov concluded that nerves in the mouth must convey a message to the brain, which then triggers the digestive reaction. He was able to show this further by severing certain nerves and observing that now the dog might eat and (without the bypass) food would reach the stomach, but no gastric juices flowed to digest the food. The brain had not received the message.

Pavlov is best known, however, for his later work on conditioned reflexes (which had a marked influence on physiologically oriented psychology in both Germany and the United States). Pavlov found that, since a dog salivates when it sees food, he could substitute another stimulus—a bell, for example—for the food and, as long as the primary stimulus (food) was associated with the secondary stimulus (bell) during a training period, the dog would salivate when it heard the bell. Pavlov supposed that new circuits of nerves developed in the cortex of the brain to allow these involuntary "conditioned" reflexes to occur.

The Birth of Cell Theory

Today the idea that living things are composed of cells seems the most basic of concepts, but before the 19th century, most biologists analyzed the makeup of animals and plants no further than the recognition that living organisms were composed of tissues and organs. As early as 1665 Robert Hooke had observed cells in cork through a microscope—and, thinking they looked like the tiny rooms in a monastery, he gave the tiny structures their name. But he had no idea that what he was looking at was part of a fundamental principle of life.

Most early observations of cells were done on plants, which are easier to see because they have cell walls, which are thicker than the cell membranes found between animal cells. With the improvement of microscopes and staining techniques (to highlight the various structures and make them more visible), scientists made more and more observations. But even in 1831, when Robert Brown discovered a small, dark structure at the center of cells and named it the "nucleus" (from the Latin word for "little nut"), neither he nor anyone else yet understood the significance of these tiny structures. In 1835 a Czech scientist named Jan Evangelista Purkinje [POOR-kin-yay] pointed out that certain animal tissues such as the skin are also made of cells. But no one paid much attention, and he did not push the point to state a full-blown theory.

Just three years later, though, in the first part of a stunning one-two punch, Matthias Jakob Schleiden [SHLY-den] (1804–81) set forth the surprising idea that all plant tissues were actually

Theodor Schwann receives credit (along with Matthias Jakob Schleiden) for the development of cell theory and histology—the study of the structure of plant and animal tissues. *(Courtesy of the National Library of Medicine)*

made of cells—that these were nature's building blocks for all plant life. The follow-up came the next year, when Theodor Schwann [SHVAHN] (1810–82) suggested that all animal tissues were also composed of cells and that an egg is a single cell from which an organism develops, that all life starts as a single cell. Since each contributed an essential part of the picture, both Schleiden and Schwann usually get the credit for the cell theory.

Others refined the details of the theory. Schleiden thought that new cells formed as buds on the surfaces of existing cells (which Mendel's nemesis, Karl Wilhelm von Nägeli, showed was not true). But cell division remained a mystery for many years. In 1845 Karl Theodor Ernst von Siebold extended the cell theory to single-celled creatures (although he thought that multi-cellular organisms were made from single-celled creatures). Also in the 1840s Rudolf Albert von Kölliker demonstrated that sperm are cells and that nerve fibers are parts of cells. The cell theory rapidly became one of the main foundations of modern biology.

Virchow and Cell Pathology

As understanding of the cell structure gained ground, researchers began to question what happened when something goes wrong with a cell. The problem became the particular passion of a man named Rudolf Carl Virchow. As a young physician in what is now Poland, he was looking into the causes of a typhus epidemic. But he could not help noticing the appalling social conditions in which his patients lived, and he spoke out frankly and passionately. It was the time of revolutionary uprisings—the year was 1848, the great year of revolutions—and the ultraconservative government of Prussia sternly put down all dissent. Virchow lost his university professorship for his stand.

But three years earlier, in 1845, he had been the first to describe leukemia, and now, in semiretirement, he had time to reflect on his ideas about the causes of the disease. The following year he found a position in Bavaria at the University of Würzburg.

Seven years later he returned to Berlin as professor of pathological anatomy, a field that he pioneered, and in 1858 he published *Cellular Pathology*, a book in which he established that cell theory extended to diseased tissue. The first cellular pathologist, he showed that diseased cells descend from normal cells. "All cells arise from

Rudolf Virchow founded cell pathology. *(Courtesy of Parke-Davis, Division of Warner-Lambert Company)*

cells," he was fond of saying, in an implicit repudiation of the idea of spontaneous generation, which maintains that living matter springs out of nonliving matter.

Given Virchow's background in the study of leukemia and cell pathology, it is not surprising that he thought disease resulted when cells revolt against the organism of which they are a part. (Though it is possible to see cancer as cells warring on cells, Virchow saw all disease this way.) As a result he resisted acceptance of an important theory put forth by the ubiquitous Louis Pasteur—a theory that implied that disease is the result of an attack by another organism.

Pasteur's Germ Theory

Of Louis Pasteur (1822–95), the prolific science writer Isaac Asimov once wrote, "In biology it is doubtful that anyone but Aristotle and Darwin can be mentioned in the same breath with him." As the founder of germ theory, the instigator of the pasteurization process for sterilizing dairy foods, and the inventor of vaccine for rabies,

Pasteur's name has become a household word. Pasteur's enormous achievements resulted from a series of intense controversies in which his ego prevailed (he liked to be right) and his perseverance paid off with major breakthroughs, first in understanding the nature of fermentation (which he said was organic; his foes claimed it was inorganic) and the question of the possibility of spontaneous generation (not possible he said; possible, his foes insisted). In each case Pasteur won the day, and in the end emerged a recognition that bacteria can cause disease.

Because of Pasteur's success with the tartrate crystals in his first serious project (see chapter 2), he was already famous in his early 30s, although he was turned down for a membership in the Académie des Sciences in 1857. He did, however, accept an appointment as dean of the Faculty of Sciences at the University of Lille. There the wine and beer industry had a problem with their products going sour, and Pasteur was asked for his help. So began Pasteur's inquiry into

Louis Pasteur, one of the greatest biologists of all time, established germ theory, a breakthrough that held major importance, not only for the study of biology, but also for health science and medicine. *(Courtesy of Parke-Davis, Division of Warner-Lambert Company)*

Shutting Out Germs

By mid-century, even before Pasteur's discoveries, a few physicians had begun to recognize that doctors could carry disease and infection between patients, although they didn't know exactly by what means.

Ignaz Philipp Semmelweiss (1818–65), a Hungarian physician trained at the University of Vienna and working in hospitals there, became concerned about an unsettling fact: Women giving birth in hospitals were dying in droves of a disease known as childbed fever, while among those who gave birth at home far fewer contracted the disease. Doctors, he became sure, were carrying the disease from patient to patient, and he ordered all the doctors under him to use a strong chemical solution to wash their hands between patients. The doctors grumbled—no doubt unhappy with the suggestion that they were causing, not curing, disease in their own patients. But they did it, and the incidence of childbed fever dropped off dramatically.

But in 1849 Hungary staged an unsuccessful revolt against the Austrian Empire (of which it formed a part), and, as a Hungarian, Semmelweiss was forced to leave his post in Vienna. The Viennese physicians went back to their old ways, skipping the unpleasant hand-washing routine, and the childbed fever deaths among their patients climbed high again—only showing that Semmelweiss was probably on the right track.

Meanwhile, wherever he worked, Semmelweiss continued to insist on his procedure, and he was able to reduce the number of childbed fever deaths among patients under his care to 1 percent. He could show that hand washing worked, but no one had yet shown that it was working because dangerous germs were being destroyed. Ironically Semmelweiss died of childbed fever from a wound he inflicted on himself while working on a patient, but he had paved the way for the work of another perceptive physician, Joseph Lister.

Joseph Lister (1827–1912) was interested in amputations—a method that promised to save lives in many instances, such as when gangrene had set in. But much too often—in 45 percent of the cases—a physician would complete an operation successfully only to see the patient die from infections afterward. In 1865 he heard about Pasteur's research in diseases caused by microorganisms, and he came up with the idea of killing germs with chemical treatment. He began using an antiseptic solution known as carbolic acid (phenol) to clean instruments in 1867. He also sprayed the air in the operating rooms and insisted on hand washing and clean aprons. The surgical death rate dropped from 45 percent to 15 percent. Joseph Lister had established antiseptic surgical technique and had killed the germs.

Then an American surgeon named William Stewart Halsted (1852–1922) took the antiseptic concept one step further. Why not just put a shield between the germs carried by physicians or nurses and their patients? So in 1890 Halsted became the first surgeon of major stature to use rubber gloves in surgery. Gloves could be sterilized much more drastically than the skin of the human hand; and they could be subjected to high temperatures and caustic chemicals that could eliminate the presence of even the hardiest germs. The wearing of rubber gloves instituted the first use of aseptic surgical technique (in which germs are not just killed in the operation room, as in antiseptic technique, but absent).

Semmelweiss's experience and Pasteur's germ theory had laid a foundation on which Lister and Halsted could build. As a result physicians changed their operating-room practices and many thousands of lives were saved.

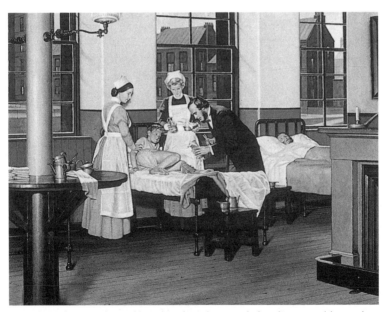

Baron Joseph Lister showed how hand washing and cleanliness could greatly reduce infections and deaths in hospitals. *(Courtesy of Parke-Davis, Division of Warner-Lambert Company)*

A man of enormous energy, Pasteur gained enormous stature in his time, leading some historians to claim that some of his successes would have been more justly awarded to others. *(Courtesy of the National Library of Medicine)*

the nature of fermentation, which he found to be a product of a certain type of living organism (a battle he won against Justus von Liebig, who had always maintained that fermentation was a purely chemical reaction, involving no living organisms). The problem was to allow the yeast organisms that produced fermentation in the wine or beer to do their job, but not let the ones that produced lactic acid (which made the beverages go sour) do their job. He suggested heating the wine and beer slightly to kill the "bad" yeast after fermentation was complete and then capping. This gentle heating process to kill undesirable microscopic organisms is now called pasteurization.

Pasteur then turned to other microscopic organisms to examine the question of where they come from. The question of spontaneous generation still haunted the study of biology. Those who believed that organisms had some vitalist essence criticized the experiments intended to show that spontaneous generation could not occur. The environment could not be hostile to life, or of course life would not occur—spontaneously or otherwise. They objected to experiments done the previous century by Lazzaro Spallanzani, in which he heated the air above the flasks of broth in which he intended to show that life could not arise from nonlife. By heating the air, they said, he had destroyed a necessary vitalist principle.

So Pasteur devised a special long-necked flask, which he sterilized. The long, thin, curved neck could be left open to allow oxygen to enter the flask, but the opening was so small that spores floating in would get caught in the bend. It worked. No organisms grew in the flask itself. But he was able to show that spores of living organisms had in fact gotten caught in the crook of the neck. He had put the question of spontaneous generation to rest at last. Now he was admitted to the Académie des Sciences.

When the silk industry in the south of France got into trouble in 1865, its leaders called the wizard, Pasteur, who quickly identified a microscopic parasite infesting the silkworms and the leaves they fed on. Destroy the infested worms and food, he said, and start afresh. The deed was done, and the silk industry was saved.

Now Pasteur turned his attention to the single greatest achievement of his career: the germ theory of disease. He began to realize that disease was communicable and that the spreading was caused by tiny, parasitic microorganisms he called "germs." (We now know "germs" are bacteria and viruses—see glossary for explanations.)

By understanding this, he realized, the method of disease communication could be stopped. He soon was advising military hospitals about sterile technique—boiling instruments and sterilizing bandages—to prevent infection and, often, avoidable death.

In the 1870s, Pasteur took on anthrax, a particularly deadly, highly communicable disease of domestic animals. In 1876 Robert Koch, a young physician in Germany, had found a germ he thought was the cause of anthrax. Using a microscope Pasteur confirmed Koch's findings and also found that the germ's spores were highly resistant to heat and could live in the ground over very long periods of time. An entire herd could become infected just by walking over the ground. Kill the affected animals, he said, burn them and bury them deep beneath the ground.

Pasteur also came up with a way to inoculate against anthrax. There was no "milder" form of the disease to use as a vaccination, as Edward Jenner had done when he had used cowpox to protect against the virulent smallpox virus. So Pasteur heated some of the anthrax germs, reducing their virulence (potential for infection), and vaccinated sheep with them, leaving some sheep unvaccinated. The unvaccinated sheep all developed anthrax and died; the vaccinated sheep did not. Seemingly unstoppable, Pasteur had developed an anthrax vaccine. He used similar methods in developing vaccines against rabies and chicken cholera.

Louis Pasteur died in 1895, having achieved enormous stature in the eyes of the world. He had won innumerable battles, most of them vast, with innovative techniques and unflappable genius. Unquestionably he was a hero in his own time and remains so to this day.

Robert Koch: Finding Causes of Disease

In the early 1870s Robert Koch (1843–1910), a young physician in a tiny town in Germany, responded to an appeal from farmers for help combating the dread anthrax epidemic that was destroying their

Sideroads of Science: Homeopathic Medicine

While Pasteur, Koch, Lister, Semmelweiss, and others began to make inroads on the causes of illness and infection, others traveled down divergent paths, not always recognizing the box canyon they were coming to at the end of the trail. Such was the case in 1796 when German physician and chemist Samuel Hahnemann (1755–1843) established the study of a medical cure he called homeopathy.

Disappointed and disillusioned by traditional medicine, Hahnemann called for eating a sound diet, getting plenty of exercise and fresh air, and dosing with extremely small amounts of naturally occurring medicines, such as herbs and barks. Most of this sounds like common sense today (except for the extremely small amounts of medication). However, in practice Hahnemann's cure was both unusual and implausible.

Hahnemann based his homeopathic medicine on three basic concepts: the law of the similars, the single medicine, and the law of infinitesimals. However, Hahnemann was not too rigorous about testing and obtaining quantitative evidence to back himself up. He was much more likely to go with his intuition.

First, similars. Hahnemann had worked with *cinchona,* the bark from a tropical evergreen tree that provides a natural source of quinine, which is used to treat malaria. However, a person who does not have malaria and takes cinchona typically comes down with malarialike symptoms. From this observation Hahnemann deduced that a medicine that produces like symptoms in a healthy patient will treat those symptoms in one who is ill, and he prescribed medications accordingly. He devised the term *homeopathic* to describe this aspect of his treatment, from the Greek *homoios* and *pathos,* or "similar sickness."

Next, the single medicine. Hahnemann may have been one of the first practitioners of "holistic" medicine, as he strove to treat the whole person,

herds of cattle. Inspired by Pasteur's work with germ theory, Koch [KOKH] was delighted by the opportunity to try to find the cause of a disease instead of just treating its symptoms. He set up a small laboratory in his home, equipped with a microscope, and began investigating blood specimens from infected cattle that had died of

not a collection of symptoms. He therefore prescribed one remedy to treat all a person's symptoms.

Finally, the law of infinitesimals—and this is where he ran into opposition from other physicians, both in his time and today. Admirably intent upon his commitment to do no harm, he strove to administer as little of a medication as possible. This seems like a laudable approach. However, the amount of medication he used, mixed with large quantities of water, was so small that it was impossible even to detect—not even one molecule remained. The solution was so diluted—an "incalculably small amount" in the dictionary definition of infinitesimal—that it was a lot like putting a drop of medicine in the Atlantic Ocean, stirring it up, and then drinking a cupful to obtain a cure.

The net results, critics maintain, are that homeopathic medicine prescribes a highly diluted amount of a "like" medicine designed to treat "the whole person," no matter what the problem is. Scientists were avidly discovering vaccines for smallpox and anthrax at the time, and vaccines are an example of "like curing like." But generally the blanket use of the principle that like cures like runs counter to the results of testing and experience. Today, for example, we know that a diabetic gets worse when eating sugar (which is found in a diseased patient's urine) and better when taking insulin (which is not a substance produced by the disease).

Today homeopathic medicine has gained new converts, attracted at least in part by the innocuous nature of the treatment and their own disenchantment with allopathic medicine and its less intuitive approach—and its apparent burden of properly conducted tests and trials before approving treatments for use in medicine. Homeopathic medicine, by comparison, seems free and unfettered—precisely because the amounts of medication are so small that the U.S. Food and Drug Administration, for example, has no jurisdiction to approve or disqualify them. Homeopathic practitioners claim that their treatments can substitute for antibiotics, some surgical procedures, and viral infections—but do not usually recommend homeopathic medicine for serious illness.

anthrax. As he looked through the lens of his microscope at the specimens, he spied rod-shaped bacilli, which he began to suspect were the culprits. (Bacilli are bacteria—see glossary.) He set out to track the entire life cycle of the bacillus, infecting mice with the disease and passing anthrax bacilli (from the blood of an infected animal) from one mouse to another through 20 generations. Shortly before, German botanist Ferdinand Cohn had observed that a bacillus forms spores and had recognized its resistance to very high temperatures. Koch now found that the anthrax bacillus forms spores that, as Pasteur also concluded, can survive in the earth for years. Koch succeeded in working out the entire life cycle of the bacillus, and Cohn enthusiastically sponsored the publication of his results.

Among Koch's many contributions to the growing understanding of the causes of infectious disease, he established rules for identifying the agent causing a disease. The researcher, he said, must locate the suspected microorganism in the diseased animal and then grow a pure strain of it in a culture. Then the cultured agent must cause the disease when introduced into a healthy animal. Also, the researcher must find the same kind of bacteria in the newly diseased animal as found in the original.

From his triumph with anthrax, Koch went on to establish improved methods for growing pure cultures of bacteria (using a gelatinous medium called agar-agar, composed from seaweed, and a culture dish invented by his assistant, Julius Richard Petri). He also succeeded in discovering the cholera bacillus and, in 1882, the tubercle bacillus, the cause of tuberculosis. His search for a cure for tuberculosis, unfortunately, met with frustration, even though at one point he thought he had found it.

In 1905 Koch received the Nobel Prize in medicine or physiology, primarily for his work on the causes of tuberculosis.

Robert Koch was a bold fighter in the search for causes of disease. *(Courtesy of the National Library of Medicine)*

PART III

Science and Society
in the Nineteenth Century

8

Pseudoscience Prospers

THE TRIUMPHS OF SCIENCE during the 18th century fanned the growing belief that science and reason could indeed be brought to bear to solve all of humanity's most vexing problems. True, some people had begun to look at science with a more critical and realistic eye, and a few more had become openly antagonistic to the scientific view of the world. Still, many continued to believe that science would ultimately lay bare the secrets not only of nature but also of philosophical questions about the human role in society and the universe.

The overriding dream many people held in the 19th century was that somehow everything in the universe—humanity and nature—shared a kind of unity. Once the key connections were discovered, answers would be revealed that would not only lead to the perfection of humans and society but would also put humanity, nature, and God into a more harmonious relationship. Two of the most popular pseudosciences of the 19th century, "spiritualism" and "phrenology," were both attempts to put science to use in improving the spiritual and social conditions of humankind.

Testimony by Bumps

Phrenology was the brainchild of Franz Joseph Gall, a Viennese physician and anatomist born in 1758. The sixth of 10 children born to Roman Catholic parents, Gall, whose father was a middle-class merchant, was educated in his childhood by Catholic schools and by his uncle, who was a priest. While Gall's parents had considered he might enter the priesthood, in 1777 at the age of 19 he traveled to Strasbourg to begin medical studies.

Some stories suggest that Gall first began to draw links during his university years between an individual's abilities and cranial characteristics. According to these stories Gall observed that some students did better than he did and he reasoned that their success was probably due to their ability to memorize facts better than he did. He also noticed that these same students appeared to have eyes that bulged outward more than normal. In a sudden, intuitive leap, he postulated that perhaps the brain's memory function was located in a particular part of the brain in the frontal lobes behind the eyeballs. Whether the story is true or not, Gall probably did begin to formulate his early ideas about what he would call cranioscopy— later known as phrenology—while attending medical school. What is known for certain is that Gall next moved from Strasbourg to Vienna to continue his medical studies, graduating in 1785.

An outgoing and popular gentleman by all accounts, Gall set up his medical practice after graduation and soon established an impressive list of eminent and wealthy clients. At the same time he began to put together a collection of an altogether different sort—a collection of human skulls. He collected authentic as well as plaster and wax models and accumulated a collection of hundreds of skulls by the end of his life. The reason for the skulls? Franz Joseph Gall had developed an idea. Although Aristotle had believed that human feelings and emotions originated in the heart, by Gall's time it was generally understood that the brain was the instrumental organ responsible for these human experiences. Pioneering work on the brain had also revealed that certain localized areas appeared to be responsible for specific functions. Combining research of his own with the research of others, along with a couple of unscientific intuitive leaps, Gall came to the conclusion that not only were all human attributes centered in the brain, but since some attributes of a person's character might be more prominent than others, the part of the brain responsible for those attributes would correspondingly be larger. Conversely, if a person exhibited a lack or diminishment of a certain trait, the corresponding section of the brain, Gall reasoned, would be smaller or less pronounced. Following this line of thought then led him to the conclusion that as a person grew and developed, the brain would shape itself in accord with the individual's temperament. Furthermore, since character is formed in early life when the human skull is more plastic and yielding, as the brain took its form beneath the skull, the skull would reflect the form of the brain. It was an audacious line of reasoning that led inevitably to Gall's next conclusion. Through careful study of numerous character

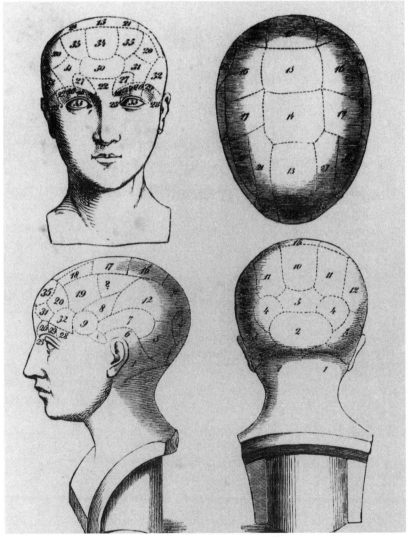

Now discredited as ineffectual, phrenology supposedly allowed a practitioner to examine a person's character and intelligence by relating expanded and diminished areas of the skull to a map showing the regions of the brain thought to govern different emotions and characteristics. *(Courtesy of the National Library of Medicine)*

traits, along with a corresponding examination of skulls, it should be possible to determine which areas of the brain were responsible for particular traits and then to develop a "map" that defined character in relation to the contours of the skull.

Physiognomy, the idea that a person's character could be revealed by the length of his nose or the set of her eyes, had been around for a long time, but with Gall's new "cranioscopy," as he called it, he claimed to be offering a new, completely "scientific" system for understanding and defining human character. In 1796 he began to offer lectures explaining his new discovery, and in 1798 he published his first detailed paper elaborating his findings.

The ball was rolling, but phrenology, the new name given to cranioscopy by Gall's young assistant Johann Caspar Spurzheim, failed to catch on widely with the general public until the idea was picked up and promoted by a Scots lawyer named George Combe (1788–1858).

Combe had attended a lecture on phrenology in Edinburgh and was quickly won over. With a lawyer's gift of language, he was soon writing a tremendously popular series of articles on the new miracle science while at the same time founding the Edinburgh Phrenological Society. Possessed of tremendous energy and a sharp awareness of the value of promotion, Combe toured extensively, giving his own lectures and making hundreds of converts. During the years 1838–40 he toured the United States giving a series of lectures entitled "The Application of Phrenology to the Present and Prospective Conditions of the United States." The somewhat ambitious theme of Combe's lectures was that America was a wonderful new social and moral experiment, and the new science of phrenology, applied correctly, could ensure the experiment's success. In short, Combe argued, the scientific understanding of individuals through phrenology would lead inevitably to a better society. Would Mr. X make an effective, honorable United States senator? Now at last, through the scientific analysis of his character using the wonderful tool of phrenology, it was possible to know. Would Miss Y be an able schoolteacher? A phrenological analysis of her character would provide the answer. Phrenology could help people find their best mates, understand their children better, aid in hiring good workers. The tour took him to just about every major city on the eastern coast and met with the same kind of success he had seen in his British tour.

Phrenology, thanks to Combe, reached the masses with a message of hope. Here at last was a science that could help people truly understand human beings, themselves as well as others. Surely with such knowledge the world could be made a better place.

Writing about Combe's book *The Constitution of Man in Relation to External Objects*, first published in 1828, the *Illustrated London News* supplement in 1858 noted, " . . . no book published within the memory of man, in the English or any other language, has effected so great a revolution in the previously received opinions of society. . . . The influence of that unpretending treatise has extended to hundreds of thousands of minds which know not whence they derived the new light that has broken in upon them, and percolated into thousands of circles that are scarcely conscious of knowing more about Mr. Combe than his name, and the fact that he was a phrenologist." The book, which went into dozens of editions, became one of the best-selling English-language books of the mid-19th century. It was said to be almost as commonly found as the Bible in many proper Victorian homes and has even enjoyed republication as recently as 1974.

If books on phrenology occupied favored places in proper Victorian homes, the trappings of phrenology also found their place in less respectable quarters of the city streets. Like most pseudosciences it was also quickly adopted by confidence tricksters, shady "fortune tellers," and quick-buck artists. Phrenology parlors sprang up in most major cities, complete with cheaply printed pamphlets and gaudy charts promising to reveal the deepest of human secrets. Sitting in a prominent position in most of these shady dens was always the famous bust, a well-marked replica of the human head complete with all its "organs" and their meanings clearly identified.

The popular masses were not the only ones, though, that bought into phrenology. Many intellectuals also found hope in it. In America it was championed by such eminent figures as the writer Ralph Waldo Emerson and the psychologist Herbert Spencer. Thomas Edison had the nooks and crannies of his head explored, Walt Whitman sang its praises, and President James Garfield announced his approval. In England the "new science" found such notable advocates as Queen Victoria, the scientist Alfred Russel Wallace, and writers such as Charlotte and Emily Brontë and George Eliot. Other admiring advocates included such notables as Karl Marx and Otto von Bismarck.

It would be misleading to suggest, though, that the vast number of scientists and intellectuals of the 19th century accepted the tenets of phrenology. By far the majority of 19th-century thinkers recog-

Phrenology practitioners performed readings by feeling the bumps on a patient's head. *(Courtesy of the National Library of Medicine)*

nized phrenology as the nonsense it was, and if they discussed it at all, spoke out heatedly against it. By 1858, the year of Combe's death and the occasion for the *Illustrated London News* article, the fad had pretty much died down. Although it continued to blossom for a few more years in America, in England the boom was over. By the 1850s, though, even in America popular attention was turning to a new wonder.

Rappings, Tappings, and Apparitions

It started in the small village of Hydesville, New York, in 1848 with an innocent practical joke played by two teenage girls, Margaret and Katie Fox.

The girls had learned the trick of secretly cracking the joints in their toes to produce curious rapping sounds. It was not difficult to convince their superstitious mother that the spirit of a recently deceased peddler was producing the raps, claiming via coded raps that he had been murdered. When word spread through the small village, the girls became local celebrities and soon the tiny Fox home became a gathering place for hopeful people petitioning the young girls to contact deceased relatives or other spirits from the beyond.

The whole thing might have remained just a local phenomenon but for the intervention of the girls' older sister Leah, who had been living in a nearby town. Quick to recognize a money-making opportunity, Leah soon scooped her younger sisters up and, after making them confess privately the truth and the tricks of their prank, she began a series of lectures and exhibitions in which the two girls demonstrated their "ability" to contact and communicate with the dead. The well-publicized performances were a tremendous success and soon scores of other so-called "mediums" (the name adopted for persons who claimed to be able to communicate with the spirits) were also displaying similar abilities.

Suddenly it seemed as if a long-closed door between the living and the dead had been opened. With that door open at last came empirical evidence that there was survival after death. While it seems strange to us today that a simple childish prank could spark a movement among literally hundreds of thousands of followers, many Americans were already prepared for just such an event—willingly and completely suppressing disbelief in the process.

Although history generally begins the chronology of the spiritualist movement in America with the Fox sisters, the way had already been paved by scores of "mesmerists" and phrenologists who had set up shop across the young nation. By then largely discredited in England and Europe, "mesmerism" claimed to heal and control human beings by way of a special force called "animal magnetism" that passed from the controller to the controlled, thus affecting the health and behavior of the person controlled. Mesmerism made the philosophical assumption that there was a natural "state" of balanced animal magnetism in every individual. Disturbance of the balance caused illness and "scientifically" controlling it allowed a person to achieve "wellness." These premises fed the optimistic American belief that science could be put to use curing all physical, spiritual, and social ills.

As a society Americans felt keenly that the new ideas of science and nature were better touchstones to truth than traditional or authoritarian tradition, and such pseudosciences as mesmerism and

Following the successes of the Fox sisters, séances became fashionable among middle-class and well-to-do society. *(© Hulton-Deutsch Collection/CORBIS)*

phrenology, with their claims to offer corroborative empirical evidence, appeared to verify the validity of their beliefs.

If the new "science" of mesmerism could heal and the new "science" of phrenology could reveal the soul's inner secrets, was it not then possible that this new "science" of spiritualism might really offer empirical evidence that the soul survived after death—and that the dead could communicate directly with the living? With so many new discoveries and innovations being revealed almost daily, and so many lecturers, philosophers, writers, and teachers loudly proclaiming the limitless powers inherent in human beings, was it not possible that even the most insurmountable barriers of the past might fall at last.

A young man named Andrew Jackson Davis broke further ground in preparing the way for the American spiritualist movement. It was Davis's achievement to add a spiritual and social dimension to the bare bones of the raps and taps of the Fox sisters and their ilk. Born in 1826 Davis, popularly known as the Poughkeepsie Seer, began making his living at the age of 14 by diagnosing illness with his so-called clairvoyant powers. Years before the teenage Fox sisters began communicating with the dead from their home in upstate New York, Davis was already holding conversations in New York City with such deceased luminaries as Emanuel Swedenborg and other spirits in "Summerland," the name he had given to the abode of souls after their departure from the Earth.

Davis, like many Americans in the mid-19th century, was convinced that America was a very special experiment and that the nation was on the verge of many major changes, social, political, and spiritual. Strongly involved in various reform movements, while he made his living by his performances and lectures, he did at least appear to firmly believe that his "powers" pointed the way to a new and a better world, whereas the Fox sisters, Margaret and Katie, under the control of their older sister, Leah, operated under a much simpler principle—take the money and run. Borrowing heavily from Swedenborgian philosophy, Davis's message of egalitarian universal love, the "natural" supernatural healing powers of human beings, and the survival of the soul after death struck a receptive chord in the psyches of many Americans who, after abandoning the rigid dogma and "moral authority" of the churches, yearned for some new empirical "truth" that would fill the void. Throughout his long life Davis attempted to fill that void by combining his religious and philosophical doctrines of spiritualism with a score of humanitarian social reform movements. At a reform convention in 1858, Davis spoke of what by then had begun to be called "spiritualism," proclaiming, "My belief in spiritualism is simply the door to my acceptance of the various reforms for which this convention has assembled . . . and I trust that to all of you Spiritualism is a broad and glorious triumphant archway leading in all directions into freedom, and a universal enjoyment of a heaven in the world."

Ironically, although in many ways Davis supplied Americans with the philosophical and religious framework that nourished the spiritualist movement, it was the popularity and publicity surrounding the Fox sisters that led so many others, for sincere reasons, as well as for less elevated ones, to become involved in the spiritualist way of life.

Becoming increasingly confused, as the movement broadened it seemed almost at times as if American egalitarianism stretched itself to the limits to try to contain the many facets of this new "science." Besides the "back parlor" mediums who used spiritualism to take a quick buck from the gullible, there was also a corresponding growth of "Spiritualist Churches" which accommodated many legitimate if misguided seekers after the new spiritual and "scientific" wisdom. It often became difficult to separate misguided but basically honest "spiritualists" from confidence tricksters. The problem became even more complicated when sincere if self-deceiving "mediums" resorted to deliberate tricks and hoaxes, justifying them as occasionally necessary to keep their followers convinced of their abilities and safely gathered within the spiritualist fold.

By the time the movement had worked its way to England, it had already become a chaotic hodgepodge. Although "spirit communication" began with the simple raps and knocks of the Fox sisters, it very quickly developed into a grotesque sideshow of attractions. Tables, chairs, lamps, and couches were moved by the spirits and jumped up and down under "spirit control." Spirits in darkened rooms and behind closed curtains played banjos, guitars, horns, and harmonicas. Mediums played ventriloquist dummies in the service of loquacious but apparently shallow-thinking dead notables such as Benjamin Franklin, Isaac Newton, William Shakespeare, and scores of American Indian warriors and chiefs. Ghostly manifestations of deceased relatives and friends materialized out of thin air. Poems, songs, concerts, and books were composed by some spirit hands while others kept themselves busy in the more mundane business of untying the hands and legs of bound mediums sitting in hastily constructed and darkened cabinets.

By 1850 a few English mediums had set up shop in London, supplemented by a handful of American arrivals. By 1853, however, spiritualist activity had grown enough to attract the interest of the British public—and the brilliant English scientist Michael Faraday. One of the first British scientists to investigate the phenomena, Faraday took a close look at the most popular activity of the early London mediums, the so-called "table tipping" phenomena. Sitting around tables in darkened rooms, the mediums would call forth spirits, who in response would tip or rock the tables under the hands of the inquiring clients, thus establishing their "spirit presence" in the darkened room. After running a number of his own experiments, Faraday published his results: The movement of the tables, he concluded, was due to the unconscious pressure on the tabletops of the sitters' hands. Faraday concluded his report with a scathing indictment of so-called educated people who accepted such nonsense as "table-tipping" and abandoned common sense and general knowledge in doing so.

It was the arrival of the young American medium Daniel Dunglas Home in 1855 that gave a kick-start to the British spiritualist movement. Home, who had built up a considerable following in America, was an interesting phenomenon in his own right. Five years before his arrival upon British shores, he had been a down-at-the-heels youth of 17. Sent to London by a group of American spiritualists, he arrived carrying a gold locket and wearing a large diamond ring and expensive clothes. All had been gifts from his admirers. Home, it seemed, had many admirers. Tall, remarkably thin, and possessed of an air of piety and almost feminine grace, he claimed an extraordinary number of spiritualist talents. Not content to be merely a passive medium through which the spirits made contact, Home possessed a much bigger bag of tricks. Among his many claimed accomplishments was his ability to elongate his body, to hold hot coals in his bare hands, and most important to levitate his body a number of feet into the air. It was an impressive bag of tricks and one that Home guarded closely, reserving them only for the well-connected and the wealthy. No paid seances ever spotted Daniel Dunglas Home's career. His talent was reserved strictly for the well-to-do patrons who invited him as a guest into their homes.

As it had in America, spiritualism began to spread in England quickly and began to serve a wide variety of interests. For some it provided an alternative religious experience and led to the formation of "spiritualist churches"; for others it was a way to alleviate the pain and sorrow of personal loss with its promise of contact with deceased loved ones; for still others it provided amusement and novelty. But for some highly educated British scholars and scientific investigators, it seemed to promise, at last, a chance to empirically prove the existence of the soul and the soul's survival after death.

The exposure and debunking of mediums had started almost from the beginning of the spiritualism movement. A local doctor looking carefully at the Fox sisters' activities even before they left Hydesville had offered his opinions, not only on the legitimacy of their claims, but on the way the mysterious spirit raps were produced.

Years later Margaret and Katie Fox confessed that the whole affair was a hoax produced by the adroit cracking of their toe joints. But long before that, the observant doctor correctly exposed the entire imposture. Yet—as has happened time after time with such "exposures" of spiritualist claims—those who wanted to believe in the claims of communication with the dead continued to believe, and those who were more skeptical simply shook their heads at the believers' gullibility. For the most part the mediums generally protested or rationalized away each exposure and continued on with their activities.

Even the true believers, though, were forced to admit that there was a great deal of fraud being practiced by mediums. There had been just too many exposures, too many times when the quick hand or eye of a skeptical sitter around the medium's table had caught the medium in the act of fraudulently producing the phenomena. Hidden assistants were caught playing the part of materialized spirits in the darkened rooms. Gimmicks were found that obviously aided in the movements of tables, chairs, and hatracks or produced glowing and floating hands and faces in the air. Professional stage magicians—who recognized many of the mediums' phenomena as simple tricks that they themselves used on stage—aided in many of the exposures. Still, despite the frauds perpetrated by "dishonest" mediums, and even occasionally by honest ones who could not always produce legitimate spirits on demand, many believers insisted that the spiritualist movement itself was legitimate. Too many phenomena had occurred that had never been explained away by skeptics, too much empirical evidence had been amassed that unequivocally proved that the soul survived death and was capable of communicating with the living.

By the late 1860s the spiritualist phenomena and the controversy surrounding it had grown significant enough that a few small groups of serious scholars and scientists decided to take a hand in the investigations.

In America one of the earliest attempts to seriously investigate the entire phenomenon of spiritualism in an organized and scientific way began in 1857 when a group of professors at Harvard University announced that they intended to start an investigation into the legitimacy of spiritualist claims of communication with the dead. To encourage mediums to come forward and allow their claims to be investigated, the *Boston Courier* offered $500 for any medium who exhibited genuine spiritualist phenomena to the satisfaction of the Harvard professors. Five mediums (including Leah Fox—Margaret and Katie's older sister—who had also begun to play the role of medium) appeared before the committee to accept the challenge. All five failed the tests. They later claimed that the conditions set up by the professors were not conducive to allowing contact with the sensitive spirits.

Generally the Harvard investigation set the scenario for future investigations. The defenders of spiritualism insisted that they had demonstrated scientifically that the souls of the dead not only survived but communicated with the living. Meanwhile they also insisted that the scientific controls and tests prepared by investigators to investigate the phenomena often discouraged the very acts that they were set up to investigate. When the testing procedures and controls were dictated, operated, and overseen by believers the reported results were positive. When the testing procedures and controls were dictated, operated, and overseen by skeptics, the results were negative. Attempts at compromise generally produced mixed results. It was not a very promising situation, and in the minds of most serious scientists, it was ludicrous, as ludicrous in the opinion of such skeptical scientists as T. H. Huxley as a group of supposedly intelligent adults sitting around a table in a darkened room thinking that they were communicating with the dead in the first place. Like the vast majority of serious scientists at the time, Huxley viewed the whole business of spiritualism as nonsense and unworthy of serious scientific consideration. When a few members of the London Dialectical

Society proposed in 1869 that the society set up a committee to investigate spiritualism, Huxley, one of the most distinguished members of the society, declined an invitation to be a part of that committee, observing that the whole thing was just so much "twaddle."

While most of us today may find the whole business as blatantly silly as Huxley did, some equally eminent 19th-century scientists such as Alfred Russel Wallace, the co-discoverer of evolution, took the whole matter with determined seriousness. One of the most active members of the committee, Wallace was predisposed toward belief in spiritualism even before the committee began its investigations, and he joined the others in issuing the committee's controversial final report.

While the committee admitted that it did not find sufficient evidence to prove the validity of communication with the dead, it did, its members claimed, find sufficient evidence to warrant continued serious investigation of the phenomena.

Read today, the report is a disturbing hodgepodge of anecdotal evidence, deeply subjective reportage, and slip-shod investigation. It did not read much better to the noncommittee members of the Dialectical Society in 1869. Much to the committee's frustration, the Dialectical Society declined to publish the final report, and the committee members were left to do so on their own.

The public reaction to the report, as can be expected, was mixed. Those who believed continued to believe, and those who were skeptical continued to be skeptical. *The Daily Telegraph* observed, "The evidence to which many witnesses set their seals is certainly extraordinary. We may be asked how we can explain all these things, and we simply reply that we cannot, and that it is not our business to do so. We are not in the presence of a sphinx that will devour us if we do not solve its enigmas. The fact, too, that some men, respectable in intellect and conversant with science, have testified their faith in the reality of the phenomena makes it worth our while to investigate the matter with keener eyes than if the believers were all impulsive and unscientific observers." Meanwhile the *Pall Mall Gazette* reported, "But for the solemnity of the witnesses, and their tediousness, their stories would read like chapters out of a handbook of natural magic. It is difficult to speak or think with anything else than contemptuous pain of proceedings such as those described in this report." *The Morning Post* demanded, "The report which has been published is entirely worthless. Is it not time that this spirit-worship ceased? We put the question seriously. With its renunciation would be swept away a vast amount of, to say the least of it, self-deception."

How could such serious scientists as Wallace participate in such a report? Was it possible, as the *Morning Post* observed, that such eminent thinkers as Wallace and his co-committee members could be guilty of such apparently obvious self-deception? A few years later, in 1873, another highly respected scientist, William Crookes, discoverer of the element thallium and the inventor of Crookes's tube (an instrument which allowed the study of cathode rays), endorsed the spirit manifestations of the medium Florence Cook. Crookes claimed that he had danced with the spirit called "Katy King," who had been materialized by Miss Cook, and even had his picture taken with the vivacious spirit.

Could self-deception stretch so far, even with a little help from the adroit deceptions of a medium and her accomplices?

The question has troubled scholars for a long time. Ideally, of course, science is a method to help you make sure that you do not fool yourself. It was the methods of science after all, that gave hope to 19th-century investigators that science could unravel the mysteries of the human "soul" and the soul's possible survival after death.

When the Society for Psychical Research (SPR) was founded by a small group of Cambridge scholars in 1882 to investigate the spiritualism phenomena, its position paper stated that the society's intention was "to approach these various problems without prejudice or prepossession of any kind, and in the same spirit of exact and unimpassioned enquiry which has enabled science to solve so many problems, once not less obscure nor less hotly debated." Writing later about the society, Henry Sidgwick, one of its founders, said, "our . . . position was this. We believed unreservedly in the methods of modern science, and we were prepared to accept submissively her reasoned conclusions, when sustained by the agreement of experts; but we were not prepared to submit with equal docility to the mere prejudices of scientific men. And it appeared to us that there was an important body of evidence—tending prima facie to establish the independence of soul or spirit—which modern science had simply left on one side with ignorant contempt; and that in so leaving it she had been untrue to her professed method and had arrived prematurely at her negative conclusions. Observe that we did not affirm that these negative conclusions were scientifically erroneous. To have said that would have been to fall into the very error we were trying to avoid. We only said that they had been arrived at prematurely. . . ." Frederic Myers, another of the society's original founders, observed about the power of science, "This method. . . . has never yet been applied to the all-important problem of the existence, the power, the destiny of the human soul."

Although certainly their intentions were pure, if a little quixotic, the fact is that most of the original members of the society passionately hoped from the beginning to find proof of the soul's existence and survival, no matter how objectively they presented their quest.

In a letter to Frederic Myers, Henry Sidgwick wrote, "I sometimes feel . . . with somewhat of a profound hope and enthusiasm that the function of the English mind, with its uncompromising matter-of-factness, will be to put the final question to the Universe with a solid passionate determination to be answered which *must* come to something."

Self-disconnected from traditional religion and religious practices, and yet still deeply yearning to discover some profound meaning to life, the original members of the SPR did not in truth begin their investigations with complete objectivity. Most had, previous to their commitment to the SPR, already developed a keen interest in such things as ghosts and so-called "haunted places."

Indicating that the SPR members had allowed themselves to participate in such "transparently childish experiments" and investigations in the first place because of their "desperate and blinding need to prove survival after death—connected perhaps with the post-Darwinian shaking of the religious foundations," critic Victoria Glendinning quotes the scholar Trevor Hall in pointing out the SPR's members' "credulous and obsessive wish . . . to believe." Hall, an expert in the history of spiritualism and the activities of the SPR, also found room to criticize the early members' "entire lack of knowledge of deceptive methods" and their feelings as sheltered English gentlemen that "respectable" people were incapable of deception.

Needless to say the first generation of SPR researchers never found or offered definite and acceptable scientific proof of either the soul or the soul's survival after death. Even before the original members began to pass from the scene, though, focus had begun to shift within the SPR as some of its most influential members gradually began to believe that many of the cases they had investigated may not have been proof of communication with the dead but may have instead been instances of so-called extrasensory perception (ESP).

Perhaps mediums were not receiving messages from the dead but were receiving messages from the sitters' minds, or through some other strange powers? Would this not also prove some special and unique qualities of human beings, some more intimate and harmonious relationship with nature and God than had ever been previously suspected? Thus focus gradually shifted within the SPR from searching for proof of the soul's survival after death to the investigation of ESP and other aspects of the paranormal, such as clairvoyance.

Although spiritualism continued into the first quarter of the 20th century and still exists in diverse forms to some degree today, its heyday was over by the end of the 19th century. The shifting attitude of the SPR in some ways foreshadowed the end of spiritualism as a movement. As more and more mediums were publicly exposed in fraud, the majority of the public began to lose interest, while investigators followed the lead of the SPR and began to split into separate factions. A few investigators continued to pursue the "spiritual" aspects of mediums—were they really talking with the dead? But many more had begun to pursue the theory of extrasensory perception—were "natural psychic powers" being consciously or unconsciously applied? As the century turned and science became increasingly professional with its insistence on "hard data," repeatability of experimentation, and skeptical verification, many people too were beginning to realize that its successes in the materialistic domain of nature did not necessarily transfer to the more ambiguous domains of the social and metaphysical realms.

9
American Commitment to Science

AS THE 19TH CENTURY OPENED, the United States of America was just over a decade old. Yet from colonial times a tradition in support of science already existed when the U.S. government first convened in New York City in 1789. American statesman Benjamin Franklin was world renowned not only for his acumen as a diplomat but also for his early successful experiments in electricity. Largely because of Franklin's friendship with British chemist Joseph Priestley—whom he had met during his travels in England—Priestley chose to emigrate to the United States in 1794 after his pro-revolutionary politics made England unsafe and unpleasant. Priestley, who is recognized as the discoverer of oxygen and the key roles it plays in both combustion and respiration, built a house and laboratory in Pennsylvania and lived there for the rest of his life.

Legacy from the Colonies

Spearheaded by the ubiquitous and energetic Mr. Franklin, a small group of dedicated scientists and individuals interested in ideas and knowledge formed the first American scientific society well before the colonies waged the Revolutionary War to win independence from England. As Franklin wrote in 1743, "The first drudgery of settling new colonies is now pretty well over, and there are many in every province in circumstances that set them at ease, and afford leisure to cultivate the finer arts, and improve the common stock of knowledge." The American Philosophical Society was formed that same year. The group boasted many of the founders of the nation, including Thomas Jefferson, George Washington, John Adams, Alexander Hamilton, Thomas Paine, Benjamin Rush, James Madison, and John Marshall. The honor of membership was also awarded to individuals from other countries who were distinguished in science and scholarly pursuits—including Antoine Lafayette of France, whose expertise in chemistry was known worldwide; Ekaterina Dashkova, director of the Russian Academy of Sciences; and in the 19th century, such luminaries as Charles Darwin and Louis Pasteur.

Franklin outlined the scope of the society's interests in broad terms, recommending pursuit of "all philosophical Experiments that let Light into the Nature of Things, tend to increase the Power of Man over Matter, and multiply the Conveniencies or Pleasures of Life." (The word *philosophical* in the 18th century meant "pertaining to all learning," most particularly the study of nature, including virtually all of what we now think of as scientific and technological pursuits.)

The society was active and growing in numbers each year right up until the revolution. Through studies and learning about agriculture, manufacturing, and transportation, its members substantially contributed to the strength of the colonial economy and helped set the stage for economic independence. The society earned international acclaim when its members participated in the coordinated observation of the transit of Venus (when the planet was seen to cross the disk of the Sun), recorded worldwide by teams of scientists in 1769.

After a brief hiatus following the war, the society was able to construct its own building on land deeded by the state of Pennsylvania, and received a charter from the state granting the right to exchange scientific information internationally whether at war or not—a principle of scientific communication that remains centrally important to this day. This tenet lies at the heart of an identification of coinciding interests between the free pursuit of science and the importance of freedom in society and government.

By 1803 the United States had elected its third president, Thomas Jefferson, who engineered the purchase of a vast expanse of land from France—the Louisiana Territory. It extended north from what is now the state of Louisiana and west from the Mississippi River,

Dashkova: First Woman in the American Philosophical Society

Born in St. Petersburg, Russia, Ekaterina Romanovna Dashkova (1743–1810) enjoyed a favored position by birth as a member of the influential Vorontsov family. She also had powerful godparents—the Empress Elizabeth and the empress's nephew and adopted son, the future Peter III. She married Prince Mikhail Ivanovich Dashkov in 1759, but his sudden death in 1764 left Dashkova and her three children on an unsound financial footing.

In the meantime she and the future Peter III's wife Catherine became friends. When Peter acceded to the throne upon Elizabeth's death in 1762, he angered powerful figures at court, in the Orthodox Church, and the army by a series of unfortunate political moves. Despite Dashkova's lifelong connection with Peter, she took part in the coup that placed his wife on the throne as Catherine II (Catherine the Great). Dashkova, only 19 years old at the time of the coup, received the Order of St. Catherine for her service.

Dashkova subsequently traveled widely in Europe, meeting Enlightenment figures such as philosopher/economist Adam Smith in Scotland, whom she visited in 1776. Upon her return to Russia in 1782, she wrote numerous published articles, including translations from French and English into Russian. The following year Catherine the Great named Dashkova head of two intellectual bodies, the Academy of Sciences (1783–96) and the Russian Academy (1783). Dashkova was responsible for placing the Academy of Sciences on a firm financial footing, and she founded several intellectual journals written in Russian and committed to topics in literature, science, and theater.

In 1789 the American Philosophical Society elected her a member of its association, having gained the sponsorship of Benjamin Franklin. She was the only new member elected in that year. Often compared with Catherine the Great, she liked to call herself Catherine the Small; however, her reputation as one of the most enlightened women of her time belies the epithet.

encompassing most of what are now known as the Midwest and Northwest states. Jefferson organized and commissioned a party of scientists and explorers, headed by Meriwether Lewis and William

In 1789 Princess Ekaterina Dashkova of Russia became the first woman to be elected to membership in the American Philosophical Society. *(Hillwood Museum & Gardens, Washington, D.C. Photo: Edward Owen)*

Clark, to explore the extent of the acquisition. To prepare for the trip that took place from 1804 to 1806, Jefferson charged the American Philosophical Society with the task of instructing Lewis and Clark

Prior to the famed expedition to explore the vast regions of the Louisiana Purchase, members of the American Philosophical Society trained Meriwether Lewis and William Clark for their duties of scientific observation and record-keeping. This drawing of a euchalon or candle fish was one of many discoveries recorded in the journals kept during the journey. *(American Philosophical Society)*

concerning the documentation of their observations of new species, geological phenomena, encounters with Native Americans and their lifestyles, practices, and languages, and so on.

Known as the Corps of Discovery, the party of 48 (at the outset) embarked from Saint Louis on one of the most exciting exploratory journeys in the nation's history—truly prepared to be a scientific expedition into a vast wilderness, home to an immense diversity of species and peoples. The journey was hard and sometimes depressing—more so than romanticized accounts usually convey—but artists for decades afterward envisioned the excitement of this vast, uncharted territory as seen for the first time by these European-American and African-American emissaries from the eastern seaboard. The West was vastly different from the East Coast—wide open plains, jagged young mountains, rushing rivers, and a gigantic ocean—and Lewis and Clark were the first to explore it scientifically and record their observations in detail.

Glimpsing the Rocky Mountains as the Lewis and Clark expedition heads west *(American Philosophical Society)*

Joseph Henry: Jump-starting American Science

In the early days of the nation's history, the American Philosophical Society in a sense had played the part of a national academy of science, along the lines of the French Académie des Sciences and the British Royal Society. It also served as a national library, museum, and patent office. In the latter half of the 19th century, its focus shifted primarily to paleontology, geology, meteorology, and astronomy, as well as American Indian ethnology.

Other scientific associations began to spring up by mid-century. The most interesting organization for the cause of science was the result of a generous bequest by British mineralogist and chemist James Smithson, himself a member of the Royal Society in London. The Smithsonian Institution, as the organization became known, had the distinction of being established by an act of Congress yet funded entirely by a bequest from outside the country. To guide the development of the institution and establish its scope and focus, the Smithsonian Board of Regents appointed Joseph Henry to the office of secretary. A fine scientist and researcher in his own right, Henry accepted the position in 1846 and became the guiding force behind its ambitious program for nearly 30 years. For many

Joseph Henry: Underrated Physicist

Joseph Henry was born in Albany, New York, in 1797. His home life was unstable, with an alcoholic father who died when Henry was 13. As a child Henry spent much of his time living with relatives and, hungry to learn but having no formal schooling, he pored over the books in the village library. During his 20s he attended the Albany Academy, and in 1826 he received a teaching position as professor of mathematics and natural philosophy at the academy.

Henry was an eager teacher and mentor, but he still found time to carry on original research on electromagnetic phenomena. He independently discovered the principle of electromagnetic induction prior to Michael Faraday's discovery of the same principle—but Faraday received official credit for the discovery because Henry had not pressed to publish his work, while Faraday did. Always evenhanded, Henry acknowledged that Faraday deserved the credit, although Henry was arguably "there first." Henry did receive credit, however, for discovering electromagnetic self-induction, a property possessed by some electrical circuits. The unit by which inductance is measured is called a "henry" in his honor. Henry also built extremely powerful electromagnets and built a prototype telegraph.

In 1832 Henry received an appointment as professor of natural philosophy at the College of New Jersey (now Princeton University), where he continued his work with electromagnetism and studied such topics as molecular cohesion, aurora, ultraviolet light, sunspots, and lightning—often perform-

"the Castle," as its main building later came to be called—from the crenellations on its towers to its stained glass windows—was home to Joseph Henry, who was the best-known and respected physical scientist in the country and whose name had become synonymous with the Smithsonian Institution.

The Smithsonian became one of the most vast, varied, and thorough-going clusters of museums and other educational programs in the world, while at the same time maintaining an impeccable orientation to research. It set a high standard under the direction of Joseph Henry and set the pace for the future.

Meanwhile several other science organizations began to form. In 1848 the American Association for the Advancement of Science was

ing highly praised demonstrations of these phenomena for his students.

Elected first secretary of the new Smithsonian Institution in 1846, he spent the rest of his life promoting the cause of science, organizing research studies, and planning the scope and focus of the fledgling institution. He encouraged research in the fields of astronomy, botany, anthropology, archaeology, zoology, and geophysics, as well as organizing a volunteer system of weather watchers that became the precursor of the national weather service. The many facets of today's Smithsonian owe their inception to Joseph Henry, including its strong commitment to research and maintenance of a wide variety of archives, museums, and other programs devoted to both education and research.

Physicist Joseph Henry served as the first secretary and director of the Smithsonian Institution, from 1846 until his death in 1878. *(AIP Emilio Segrè Visual Archives)*

The Smithsonian Institution at the end of the 19th century (*The Smithsonian Institution*)

formed, emphasizing unity among the numerous disciplines that were beginning to form. Today it is the largest professional association of scientists in the world, publisher of the prestigious weekly journal *Science*.

Another act of Congress established and incorporated the National Academy of Sciences in 1863, founding a group whose purpose was to advise the federal government on issues pertaining to science and technology. By law, no compensation is given for these services (thereby hoping to avoid bias), and members are elected on the basis of their expertise and distinction as scientists or engineers.

With the founding of these organizations and other more specialized groups, a standard of professionalism in science was well established in the United States by the end of the 19th century—in the face of new and ever more complex challenges to be faced in the exciting adventure of developing a more finely honed approach to solving the mysteries of the universe.

10

The Great Age of Synthesis

We look for a bright day of which we already behold the dawn.

—Humphry Davy, in a lecture in London

ARMED WITH THE CONTINUED SUCCESS of science and its applications, scientists had greeted the 19th century with great optimism. The year 1800 marked the dawn of a time when expanding scientific knowledge and technological advancement virtually created the positive, can-do-spirit of the Victorian era that spanned the last two-thirds of the century. By the end of the century, electricity lit the streets of London, telegraph communication transformed journalism and business alike, factories hummed, and urban streets bustled with commerce.

Politically and economically, however, the sense of the time was not so monolithically positive. The 19th century was a time of alternating periods of peace and revolution, of nationalism in Europe, in the Ottoman Empire, and in the Americas, of internal struggles to liberalize the governments of Europe, of industrialization and accompanying growing pains, and of wide-ranging imperialism on the part of the countries of Europe.

The first years of the century were plagued by the expansionism and wars of France's emperor, Napoléon I (Bonaparte). In 1815, with Napoleon defeated at last, the governments of Europe met at the Congress of Vienna to reestablish peace and a balance of power in Europe. But revolutions broke out between 1820 and 1830. The year 1848 brought widespread revolution—partly as a result of the economic crises of 1846–48, caused by the great potato famine in Ireland, by a small grain harvest due to drought throughout Europe, and by the economic hard times that followed. Food shortages, high prices, and unemployment all set the stage for revolt.

In addition, many leaders had backtracked on the civil rights symbolized by the French Revolution. People were angry and hungry and tired of being powerless, and socialist ideals gained wide appeal among the workers of France. *The Communist Manifesto* written by Karl Marx and Friedrich Engels, first published in early 1848 and translated into French, added further fuel to the growing unrest. In a bloody French workers' revolt in June of that year, at least 1,500 people were killed in the uprising, as many as 8,500 were wounded, and thousands wound up in jail. But the right to vote was won for every male—not just landowners—in what constituted a major milestone in the struggle for equal rights (though voting rights for women were still a long way off). Other revolts broke out in Austria, Hungary, and Italy, as well.

Meanwhile, under the influence of industrialization and the voracious hunger it produced for cheap raw materials, worldwide imperialism became stronger. Europeans took over nearly every country in Africa by the end of the century, and Britain established sovereignty in India and a vast array of far-flung lands. The Far East, including China and Japan, was opened up to trade (not always without bloodshed).

Then, as now, science sometimes served governments in time of war, but for the most part the pursuit of science stood apart from international politics and yet was at the heart of society's economic growth and industrialization. As we have seen, the 19th century gave rise to a new kind of alliance, an international intellectual alliance of seekers of truth, that cut across national boundaries and overcame the parochial concerns of nation against nation.

The growing professionalism of science—since more and more men and women made their living by their scientific work—and the fruits of science (as well as the hazards) played an increasingly prominent role in the public mind. Geologists transformed mining. Physicists brought new insight into ways of harnessing energy. Meanwhile advances in the biological sciences made possible important breakthroughs in medicine and health science.

The Industrial Revolution, the most wide-ranging effect of scientific discovery, completely transformed the way people lived and worked in the 19th century. Begun in the 18th century, especially in England, with inventions that mechanized the production of cloth, the Industrial Revolution moved into full swing in the 19th as James Watt's steam engine (perfected in 1781) found more and more uses in industry and transportation. By 1804 Richard Trevithick, in England, had built a locomotive that pulled five loaded coaches along a track for nine and a half miles, and by 1814 the great railroad pioneer George Stephenson had introduced his first steam locomotive. Soon railroads crisscrossed England, Europe, and North America as factory production increased with the use of steam power and the demand for efficient transportation escalated. Urban centers took on more and more importance in what had once been bucolic countryside. Overall, throughout the century, science lay close to the heartbeat of all progress and acted as a catalyst of industrial and intellectual change.

Industrialization also became a tool of greed, however, and took the blame for hardships suffered by workers whose employers required them to work long hours in unsafe conditions for too little pay. Not everything about the Industrial Revolution was glorious, and those who lost jobs to new inventions and endured inhumane conditions rapidly came to resent the growth of technology and science.

But industrialization overall boosted the quality and availability of goods for an enormous number of individuals. The improvements in transportation increased mobility, connected isolated communities, and improved the flow from farm and factory to market. In England in particular, improved economic conditions brought new opportunities and a better quality of life, especially for the middle class.

Science, as a result, loomed large in the public mind, and from the mid-1830s on, lectures on science became enormously popular. In late November 1859, Charles Darwin's *On the Origin of Species* sold out on the first day of its publication. Associations and societies for those interested or engaged in science sprang up, not just in the United States, but everywhere. An organization known as the British Association for the Advancement of Science was founded in 1831, and a man named William Whewell coined the word *scientist* in 1833, replacing *natural philosopher,* to describe its members.

This was the era in which science and scientists came of age. Experimental approaches and procedures became much more complicated (a trend that has continued into the 20th century), to the point

Charles Darwin struggled with the bitterness of his oldest daughter's death and could not reconcile the tragic loss with a belief in a just and loving God. *(Edgar Fahs Smith Collection—University of Pennsylvania Library)*

that by the end of the century, the era of the amateur scientist had ended. For the first time, out of necessity, scientists were primarily full-time professionals, usually specialists, not part-time amateurs or generalists. They began to need outside financial support even just to obtain the equipment for their experiments. And they required formal training to keep up with their fields, which became more and more specialized into specific disciplines such as chemistry, physics, astronomy, biology, and subdisciplines such as organic chemistry and genetics.

Scientists also began to specialize between theorists and experimentalists, especially in the physical sciences. This was not an entirely new trend. Johannes Kepler, the great astronomer-theorist of the 17th century, had stood on the shoulders of Tycho Brahe, the great astronomical observationist who had collected the mountains of data from which Kepler drew his conclusions. Isaac Newton, the great synthesizer, stood on the shoulders of Galileo, the experimenter. But now, in the 19th century, the interplay of experimentalist and theorist soon became even more pronounced. And the roles of experimenter and theorist soon rarely resided in the same person— there was simply too much to be done, too broad a swath to cut. And the approaches required became vastly different—too different, as a rule, to reside comfortably in the same personality. How many people could possess both the fastidious attention to detail and tenacious perseverance required of a good experimenter and, at the same time, the theorist's ability to think broadly and abstractly, juxtaposing seemingly unrelated concepts, and interpreting and synthesizing results?

It was also a time of increasing complexity in the substance of science—not just in specific disciplines such as chemistry, physics, astronomy, biology, psychology, and organic chemistry. The fields of chemistry and geology in particular reached a new maturity after the striking advances of the previous century. The boundaries between the sciences became more or less set, and the almost "Renaissance"-like, multidisciplinary approaches of 18th-century investigators like Joseph Priestly, René Descartes, and Benjamin Franklin gave way to specialization. In the 1830s John Herschel could still choose to be a generalist, making contributions not only in astronomy but in chemistry and mathematics as well. But he was already an exception to the rule. Science had become too complex for an individual to make significant contributions without going deeply into a single area or discipline.

Yet the 1800s were also a great time of synthesis in the sciences. From the time of the Greeks, scientists have looked for a few simple, underlying principles to explain the seemingly unrelated, complex details of the physical universe and the living organisms that inhabit it. By the 19th century the idea of convergence had become paramount. Strong indications had begun to emerge that seemed to hint that everything might be explained by just a few explanatory theories—if indeed not by just one.

Physicists, especially, had already had more than a taste of evidence that everything might soon converge into one. Isaac Newton had shown in the 17th century that the same force causes the fall of an apple in an orchard and the periodicity of the Moon, two events that seemed at first glance (and had for many centuries) not to be remotely related. Benjamin Franklin, in the 18th century, had shown that the static shock one might get from an iron railing was related to lightning in the thunderclouds overhead.

"I wish we could derive the rest of the phenomena of nature by the same level of reasoning from mechanical principles," wrote Newton, "for I am inclined by many reasons to suspect that they may all depend on certain forces."

The scientists of the 19th century were primed to find even more convergence than Newton probably meant to suggest, to come up with even more all-encompassing ideas. And they did.

Atomism, which came of age in the early 1800s under the direction of John Dalton, was above all a reductionist idea—the desire to reduce all the complex forms of matter occurring in nature to a few fundamental particles that respond to a few basic laws.

By 1800 Alessandro Volta had put together his "voltaic cell," the first usable battery. Before his invention, scientists could neither really study electricity nor use it, because they could only get fleeting glimpses of small amounts of static electricity or momentary discharges. Now they had an electric current. Then Hans Christian Ørsted made his accidental discovery that electricity and magnetism were linked and published his discovery in 1820. Major breakthroughs tumbled one after the other out of the laboratories and calculations of Michael Faraday, André Marie Ampère, and others. In a striking example of how a new scientific tool can uncork a bottleneck, much of the 19th-century science flowed from the electromagnetic theory that followed and from the use of electrolysis in chemistry.

The stunning idea that electricity, magnetism, and light were all forms of the same energy force galvanized the world of physics. In fact, energy, investigators found, could be transformed into many different forms: heat, mechanical motion, electricity, light. Many scientists believed that energy would be the great unifying theme of the century—that the answer to everything, ultimately, would boil down to one unifying theory of energy. So much progress was made in the 1800s, in fact, that many physicists believed that only a few problems remained to be solved. The study of physics, they claimed, would soon come to an end—since not much was left to discover. (They were not right, of course.)

Great, all-encompassing ideas were not confined to the physical sciences, either. In biology there was the extraordinary set of principles set forth by Charles Darwin and Alfred Russel Wallace to explain how so many diverse species came to form. With each new voyage to far-away, isolated lands, the sheer enormous diversity of life became ever more mind-boggling. Yet

Alessandro Volta's simple battery cell opened the doors to a revolution inspired by electricity—a revolution that continues yet today. *(Edgar Fahs Smith Collection— University of Pennsylvania Library)*

the theory of evolution could provide viable explanations for it all. Moreover, Gregor Mendel's law of genetics offered new insights into how traits were passed on from one generation to another.

However, not everyone believed that unity in science would come through convergence of theories. Some, like James Clerk Maxwell, thought instead that the sciences would be unified by methods of approach, not by any one theory (strangely enough, since he was the author of electromagnetic theory, one of the great unifying concepts of all time). In England, especially, the most frequently used method was the idea of using an analogy, or model, to represent how a concept worked. (The French tended to think that the approach was childish and simplistic, but in England, scientists of varied backgrounds found that a fountain of ideas flowed from building a mechanical model. Dalton, Faraday, William Thomson, and Maxwell all found models enormously fruitful.)

The 19th century also saw the demise of alchemy and its mysticism, which had dogged much progress, especially in chemistry, for many preceding generations. No longer did chemists speak, by the end of the century, of a mysterious group of substances known to their predecessors as "imponderables." For the previous century this vestige of alchemy had dominated almost every effort to get at the nature of reactions that took place when substances were combined or when combustion took place. Heat, light, magnetism, and electricity were all thought to be weightless fluids that transferred from one substance to another. Their presence could not be detected by weight because they had no weight. Lavoisier had discredited the theory of "phlogiston," another imponderable postulated to explain combustion, but the rest of the imponderables remained part of scientific theory until, in the 19th century, one by one, discoveries led to sounder explanations of the way things worked. And the last traces of mysticism finally dropped away from scientific inquiry.

As scientific ideas became more powerful and cohesive, controversy swirled around them. Some criticized the rejection of long-held beliefs, including alchemy, mysticism, and astrology. Many balked at new theories—Darwin and Wallace's theory of evolution, in particular—that seemed to compete with biblical accounts and overthrew the long accepted hierarchy that set humans apart from the rest of the animal world.

Several influential factions of European society also opposed science outright as anticreative, rigid, and constrictive. In Germany the

French philosopher Jean-Jacques Rousseau spearheaded the romantic movement just before the 19th century began. *(Stock Montage Inc.)*

scientist-poet Johann Wolfgang von Goethe and the philosopher Georg Hegel became arch-opponents of what they termed the mechanistic and materialistic nature of science, and the idealistic and romantic German *Naturphilosphie* gained popularity toward the end of the 18th and beginning of the 19th century. In France, following the restoration of the Bourbons in 1814, antiscientific romanticism became the socially popular stance to take, derived from seeds sown in the 18th century by the eloquent French philosopher Jean-Jacques Rousseau. A contributor to the rationalist *Encyclopédie* (Encyclopedia), in later years Rousseau embraced romanticism's defense of intense subjective experience in preference to rational thought.

Such prestigious 19th-century writers as Anne-Louise-Germaine de Staël (often referred to as Mme de Staël [du-stah-EL]) and René de Chateaubriand [sha-TOH-bree-anh] scorned the "whole brood of mathematicians," and the French poet Alphonse de Lamartine, intoxicated over the power of human emotion, wrote loftily, "Mathematics were the chains of human thought. I breathe, and they are broken." The romantics saw human feeling and individualism as the source of all creative power, and they saw the universe as an organism, not a machine. They set the subjectivity of the "heart" and imagination in opposition to the more objective fruits of the scientific mind. The English poet John Keats spoke for many romantics when he wrote that he was "certain of nothing but the holiness of the heart's affections, and the truth of imagination. What the imagination seizes as beauty must be truth . . ."

The intense controversy over evolutionary theory stood as an example of the deeply rooted beliefs with which science had begun to cross swords. Many people became uneasy at the implications of

Charles Darwin's account that the diverse species in nature had evolved from common ancestors through natural selection. Nearly every conservative paper in England ran cartoons lampooning Darwin and his ally, T. H. Huxley, as apes, monkeys, or gorillas. But the attention given issues like this in the press marked the high level of significance they had in the popular mind.

Long past were the days of Copernicus, in the 16th century, when only a few educated scholars had any hope of following the arguments set forth by science, let alone any interest. These were exciting times, when science, or at least a public persona of science, held a center-stage spotlight for all to see. It was a spotlight whose intensity increased as the years—and discoveries—rolled forth.

Conclusion
How Much Remains Unknown

Fortunately science, like that nature to which it belongs, is nei-ther limited by time nor space. It belongs to the world, and is of no country and no age. The more we know, the more we feel our ignorance; the more we feel how much remains unknown . . .

—Humphry Davy on November 30, 1825

THE 19TH CENTURY WAS A GIANT ERA in the history of science, a time when major discoveries opened up new worlds to explore—the worlds of atomic theory and dozens of new elements; of ther-modynamics, electricity, and electromagnetism; of diverse, evolving species and dinosaur bones; of plant and animal cells and of tiny, pathological organisms. New tools and methods such as electrolysis and spectroscopy provided keys to the elements, the stars, and the universe. Scientists learned from each other (as Faraday did from Davy, and Maxwell did from Faraday), vied with each other for pri-ority (as Davy did with nearly everyone), were gracious with each other (in the manner of Darwin and Wallace), and argued issues assiduously (as Huxley did with Lyell, Agassiz, and others). It was a time when science at last came into its own as a profession.

But by the end of the century, the very fabric of science was on the brink of change. What for Dalton, Faraday, Le Verrier, Maxwell, and Helmholtz had seemed a noble pursuit of absolutes, of ultimate truths, was about to shift mightily. In the 1890s, as a new genera-tion was about to take the helm—the generation of Max Planck, Ernest Rutherford, Marie Curie, Wilhelm Roentgen, Niels Bohr, and Albert Einstein—certain absolutes seemed firm: Newtonian mechanics with its three-dimensional space and linear time, the laws of thermodynamics, Maxwell's electromagnetic waves in all-pervading ether. But the dawn of the 20th century would bring extraordinary, mind-boggling change to all of these. So far only the tip of the iceberg of science had been touched.

When Max Planck began the study of physics in the late 1870s, one of his teachers advised him not to go into the field—a few loose ends remained, he was told, but on the whole, all the major discoveries had already been made. But, as it has turned out, science is truly as limitless as the time and space it examines, and the words Humphry Davy spoke in 1825 held no less true at the end of the century than at the beginning—and they still hold true to this day.

CHRONOLOGY

The 19th Century

1800

▶ Allessandro Volta announces his invention (invented the previous year) of an electric battery
▶ William Herschel detects infrared light

1801

▶ Johann Ritter discovers ultraviolet light
▶ Giuseppe Piazzi discovers Ceres
▶ Georges Cuvier identifies 23 species of extinct animals, adding fuel to the argument about the permanency of species

1802

▶ Thomas Young develops the wave theory of light

1803

▶ After studying meteorites found in France, Jean-Baptiste Biot argues that the strange "stones" did not originate on Earth

1804

▶ Richard Trevithick builds a locomotive that pulls five loaded coaches along a track for 9.5 miles
▶ Napoleon I crowns himself emperor of the French

1805

▸ Joseph-Marie Jacquard develops the Jacquard loom. To control the operation of the loom, Jacquard uses a system of punched cards, an idea that will later be incorporated in the design of early computers

1807

▸ Robert Fulton builds the steamship *Clermont*
▸ Coal-gas lights begin to illuminate the streets of London

1808

▸ Humphry Davy develops the first electric-powered lamp
▸ *The New System of Chemical Philosophy* by John Dalton revolutionizes chemistry

1809

▸ Jean-Baptiste de Monet, chevalier de Lamarck publishes *Zoological Philosophy*

1810

▸ Davy shows that chlorine is an element

1811

▸ Amedeo Avogadro proposes his hypothesis, now known as Avogadro's law, which states that equal volumes of gases contain an equal number of molecules under identical conditions of temperature and pressure
▸ Herschel develops his theory of the development of stars and nebulae

1812

▸ Cuvier discovers the fossil of a pterodactyl
▸ Pierre Simon de Laplace suggests that the universe can be viewed as a vast machine, and that if the mass, position, and velocity of every particle could be known, the entire past and future of the universe could be calculated

1814

- Joseph von Fraunhofer rediscovers and charts solar spectral lines
- George Stephenson introduces his first steam locomotive

1815

- Davy invents the safety lamp to be used by coal miners
- William Prout suggests that hydrogen is the fundamental atom and that all other atoms are built up from different numbers of the hydrogen atom. Prout makes his first speculation anonymously since he himself thinks that the idea may be too extravagant
- Napoleon is defeated at Waterloo
- John Louden McAdam constructs the first truly paved road

1816

- Augustin Fresnel demonstrates the wave nature of light

1817

- Fresnel and Thomas Young demonstrate that light waves must be transverse vibrations

1818

- Fresnel publishes "Memoir on the Diffraction of Light"
- Johann Franz Encke discovers what is now known as Encke's Comet
- Jöns Jacob Berzelius publishes his table of atomic weights

1819

- Hans Christian Ørsted discovers that magnetism and electricity are two different manifestations of the same force. He publishes this theory in 1820
- Pierre Louis Dulong and Alexis Thérèse Petit show that the specific heat of an element is inversely proportional to its atomic weight

1820

- The Royal Astronomical Society is founded in London

1821

▶ Michael Faraday demonstrates that electrical forces can produce motion (the first electric motor)

1822

▶ Jean-Baptiste-Joseph Fourier demonstrates Fourier's theorem and publishes his *Théorie analytique de la chaleur* (Analytical theory of heat)
▶ Charles Babbage proposes the first modern computer but does not have the necessary modern materials with which to build it

1823

▶ John Herschel suggests that the so-called Fraunhofer lines might indicate the presence of metals in the sun

1824

▶ Nicolas Léonard Sadi Carnot publishes "On the Motive Power of Fire"
▶ The first school for science and engineering opens in the United States. It will eventually become the Rensselaer Polytechnic Institute

1825

▶ George Stephenson builds an improved steam locomotive

1827

▶ Georg Simon Ohm proposes what is now called Ohm's law
▶ Robert Brown reports his observation of the phenomenon now called "Brownian motion," which years later would help scientists to offer further proof of the existence of atoms

1828

▶ Friedrich Wöhler synthesizes urea, offering proof against the vitalist view that only living tissue could create organic molecules

1830

▶ Charles Lyell publishes the first volume of *The Principles of Geology,* offering evidence for the uniformitarian theory of the Earth's geological history

1831

▶ Charles Darwin begins his five-year voyage aboard the *Beagle,* on which he takes along the first volume of Lyell's boo

▶ Michael Faraday discovers electromagnetic induction and devises the first electric generator. The discovery is made almost at the same time by American scientist Joseph Henry

1832

▶ Faraday announces what are now called the laws of electrolysis

1833

▶ At a meeting of the British Association for the Advancement of Science, William Whewell proposes the term *scientist*

1834

▶ Cyrus Hall McCormick patents the McCormick Reaper

1835

▶ Gaspard Gustave Coriolis announces the "Coriolis effect"

1837

▶ Darwin begins to put together his theory of evolution but does not publish

1838

▶ Friedrich Bessel announces first precise measurements (using parallax) of the distance to a star

▶ Matthias Jakob Schleiden announces his theory that all living plant tissue is made up of cells

1839

▶ Theodor Schwann extends Schleiden's cell theory to animals as well

▶ Louis Jacques Mandé Daguerre invents the daguerreotype, an early type of photography

1840

▶ John William Draper takes the first photograph of the Moon

▶ Germain Henri Hess founds the science of thermochemistry

1842

▸ Christian Johann Doppler points out the phenomena of sound and other emissions from moving sources now known as the "Doppler shift"

1843

▸ Samuel Heinrich Schwabe announces his discovery of the cyclic action of sunspots. The discovery begins early work in solar physics and astrophysics

1844

▸ Samuel F. B. Morse patents his design for the telegraph

1846

▸ The planet Neptune is discovered by Urbain Jean Joseph Le Verrier
▸ The Smithsonian Institution is founded in America

1847

▸ Hermann von Helmholtz proposes the law of the conservation of energy (first law of thermodynamics), which states that heat is a form of energy and energy is conserved

1848

▸ Lord Rosse discovers the Crab Nebula
▸ *The Communist Manifesto* by Karl Marx and Friedrich Engels is published; revolutions sweep Europe

1849

▸ Jean Léon Foucault detects spectral emission lines

1850

▸ James Prescott Joule publishes his final figure for the mechanical equivalent of heat
▸ Rudolf Clausius becomes the first scientist to describe clearly the second law of thermodynamics, which states that heat does not flow spontaneously from cold to hot objects

- W. C. Bond of Harvard University makes the first astronomical photograph

1851

- William Thomson (later to be known as Lord Kelvin) proposes the concept of absolute zero
- The Great International Exhibition opens in London, promoting the application of science to technology
- Foucault demonstrates the rotation of the Earth

1852

- Edward Frankland publishes his theory of what came to be called "valence" in chemistry
- Elisha Graves Otis builds the first safety elevator

1853

- Helmholtz proposes ideas about the ages of the Sun and the Earth based on his studies of the conservation of energy

1855

- Robert Bunsen and Gustav Kirchhoff begin work on the basics of spectral analysis

1856

- First skeleton of what we now call Neandertals (sometimes spelled Neanderthals) is found in a cave in Neander Valley, Germany
- Henry Bessemer develops the "Bessemer process" and begins to build new "blast furnaces" that will open up the era of inexpensive steel
- Louis Pasteur develops what is now known as "pasteurization," a process for heating a liquid (especially milk) sufficiently to kill bacteria without changing flavor, composition, or nutrition

1858

- Darwin and Alfred Wallace announce their theory of evolution by natural selection to the Linnaean Society
- Rudolf Virchow publishes *Cellular Pathology*
- The first transatlantic telegraph cable is laid

1859

- Darwin's *On the Origin of Species* is published
- Edwin Drake drills first oil well near Titusville, Pennsylvania
- Gaston Plante develops first storage battery
- Kirchhoff and Bunsen announce their ideas on spectral lines

ca. 1860

- James Clerk Maxwell develops the kinetic theory of gases, relating motion in molecules to the measurable characteristics of a gas, such as temperature and pressure. Ludwig Boltzmann also develops the theory independently and publishes his papers in the 1870s

1860

- Pasteur adds final argument against the long-held but increasingly shaky theory of spontaneous generation, the idea that some life forms arise spontaneously from nonliving matter
- Pierre Berthelot's work in synthesizing such organic molecules as methyl alcohol, ethyl alcohol, and methane adds further proof of the ability of chemists to synthesize organic molecules from the elements, thus adding another blow to vitalist theories, which held that studying chemical and physical phenomena cannot lead to an understanding of the nature of life
- Stanislao Cannizzaro wins chemists over to Avogadro's hypothesis with his speech and pamphlet at the First International Chemical Conference at Karlsruhe
- Kirchhoff suggests that a body that absorbed all light and reflected none (called a black body) would, when heated, emit all wavelengths of light. This simple idea leads to questions that will help open up the next great revolution in physics in the early days of the 20th century

1861

- San Francisco and New York City are connected by a telegraph line

1862

- Foucault offers a new estimate for the velocity of light
- Pasteur publishes his evidence for his germ theory of disease

1863

▸ The National Academy of Sciences is founded in the United States
▸ William Huggins, after studying the spectra of some bright stars, announces that their spectral lines are those of familiar elements

1864

▸ Huggins, making the first spectrum analysis of a nebula, proposes that it is composed of gas

1865

▸ Gregor Mendel's theory of dominant and recessive genes is published in a little-known journal and goes unnoticed until the early 1900s
▸ Clausius coins the term *entropy,* describing the degradation of energy in a closed system

1867

▸ Marx publishes *Das Kapital*
▸ The first truly functional typewriter is developed by Christopher Sholes

1868

▸ Helium is discovered by Pierre Jules César Janssen while he is studying the spectral lines of the sun
▸ The first known Cro-Magnon skeletons are discovered in a cave in France

1869

▸ The Suez Canal opens
▸ Dmitry Mendeleyev publishes his "periodic table of the elements"
▸ The final spike is driven to complete the first transcontinental railway line in America

1870

▸ The businessman and amateur archeologist Heinrich Schliemann discovers the ancient city of Troy, uncovering vast amounts of gold and valuable objects and making the study of archeology a part of the popular consciousness

1871

▶ Darwin publishes *The Descent of Man*

1872

▶ Henry Draper is the first to photograph the spectra of a star

1873

▶ Maxwell publishes his theory of electromagnetism, the unification of theories of electricity and magnetism, predicting the existence of electromagnetic waves and recognizing light as an electromagnetic phenomenon

1875

▶ Sir William Crookes develops the radiometer

1876

▶ Alexander Graham Bell patents the telephone
▶ Nikolaus August Otto develops the four-cycle engine, the basis for today's internal-combustion engines
▶ Josiah Willard Gibbs applies the theory of thermodynamics to chemical change
▶ Repeating the work done by Julius Plücker almost two decades before, Eugene Goldstein describes the phenomena of cathode rays and is the first to use the term

1877

▶ Thomas Alva Edison invents the phonograph

1879

▶ Albert Michelson determines the velocity of light
▶ Edison invents the incandescent electric lightbulb

1880

▶ Herman Hollerith develops the first electromechanical calculator. It is the next step toward today's modern computers

1882

▶ In America the Pearl Street Power Station brings electric lighting to New York City

1884

▶ Ottmar Mergenthaler patents the Linotype machine

1885

▶ Carl Friedrich Benz develops the first working automobile with a gasoline-burning internal-combustion engine

1887

▶ Albert Michelson and Edward Morley attempt to measure the changes in the velocity of light produced by the motion of Earth through space. Their failure to find any changes leads to the abandonment of belief in the ether and helps open the doorway to 20th-century physics
▶ Heinrich Rudolph Hertz makes the first observation of the photoelectric effect; his observations will prove of great importance to the physics of the coming century

1888

▶ Hertz produces and detects radio waves and gives experimental evidence for the electromagnetic theory of Maxwell

1889

▶ The Eiffel Tower is finished in Paris. At the time it is the world's tallest human-made freestanding structure
▶ Edward Charles Pickering makes the first observations of spectroscopic binary stars

1890s

▶ Edison, borrowing on the ideas of others, develops the first successful motion pictures

1894

▶ The discovery of "Java Man" is announced by Marie Eugène Dubois

1895

▶ Sir William Ramsay discovers the element helium on Earth and finds that it would lie between hydrogen and lithium in the periodical table
▶ Edward Emerson Barnard photographs the Milky Way
▶ Wilhelm Konrad Röntgen discovers X-rays

1896

▶ Antoine Henri Becquerel discovers natural radioactivity

1897

▶ J. J. Thomson discovers the electron

1898

▶ Marie and Pierre Curie isolate the radioactive elements of radium and plutonium

GLOSSARY

atom   The basic unit of an element; originally, as conceived by Democritus, the smallest, indivisible particle of a substance

atomic weight   A number representing the weight of one atom, usually expressed in relationship to an arbitrary standard. Today the isotope of carbon taken to have a standard weight of 12 is commonly used, but several other standards were also used in the 19th century

bacteria   (singular: bacterium)   A large and varied group of micro-organisms, typically single-celled. They are found living in many different environments, and they typically have no chlorophyll, multiply by simple division, and can be seen only with a micro-scope. Some bacteria cause diseases such as pneumonia, tuber-culosis, and anthrax, while others are necessary for fermentation and other biological processes

caloric   Term used to describe heat as a fluid, common in the 18th century, used by Antoine Lavoisier, among others

calx   Term used in the 18th and 19th century for oxidized metal (which we would call "rust"); originally the Roman name for lime, which Humphry Davy discovered was oxidized calcium

cell   The basic unit of all living organisms; a very small, complex unit of protoplasm, usually organized in large numbers

compound   A substance formed when two or more atoms of different elements are chemically united

diffraction   The breaking up of a ray of light into dark and light bands or into the colors of the spectrum

electrochemistry   The science of the interaction of electricity and chemical reactions or changes

electrolysis   Chemical change produced in a substance by the use of electricity; used especially to analyze substances

electromagnetism   Magnetism caused by electrical charges in motion; the physics of electricity and magnetism

element   A substance that cannot be broken down into simpler substances

entropy   A measure of the degree of disorder in a substance or a system; entropy always increases and available energy diminishes in a closed system

evolution   The theory that groups of organisms may change over a long period of time so that descendants differ from their ancestors

inert gas   A gas that has few or no active properties and does not react with other substances

isomers   Chemical compounds that have the same composition and molecular weight (the same chemical formula) but differ in the arrangement of atoms within the molecules and have different chemical or physical properties

mixture   A blend of substances not chemically bound to each other

molecule   Two or more atoms chemically bound together, the fundamental particle of a compound

natural selection   The process by which those individuals of a species with characteristics that help them adapt to their specific environment tend to leave more progeny and transmit their characters, while those less able to adapt tend to leave fewer progeny or die out, so that there is a progressive tendency in the species to a greater degree of adaptation. The mechanism of evolution discovered by Charles Darwin

parallax   An apparent shift in position of an object viewed from two different locations, for example, from Earth at two different positions on opposite sides of its orbit (achieved by observing the objects at six-month intervals). The greater the apparent change in position, or "annual parallax," the nearer the star

pneumatic   Having to do with gases

polarize   To produce polarization, that is, the condition of light or radiated energy in which the orientation of wave vibrations is confined to one plane or one direction only

refraction   The bending of a ray or wave of light (or heat or sound) as it passes obliquely from one medium or another of different density, in which its speed is different, or through layers of different density in the same medium

thermodynamics   The physics of the relationships between heat and other forms of energy

virus   The smallest form of living organism, composed of nucleic acid and a protein coat; one of a group of ultramicroscopic or submicroscopic infective agents that cause various diseases in animals, such as measles, mumps, and so on, or in plants, such as mosaic diseases. Viruses cannot replicate without the presence of living cells and are regarded both as living organisms and as complex proteins

vitalism   The doctrine that the life in living organisms is caused and sustained by a vital force that is distinct from all physical and chemical forces. Kekulé's description of organic molecules as those containing carbon, with no reference to a life force or living matter, was a blow against the doctrine of vitalism

wavelength   In a wave, the distance from one crest to the next, or from one trough to the next

FURTHER READING
AND WEB SITES

About Science in General

Cole, K. C. *First You Build a Cloud: And Other Reflections on Physics as a Way of Life*. San Diego, Calif.: Harvest Books, 1999. Well-written, lively look at physics presented in a thoughtful and insightful way by a writer who cares for her subject.

Gardner, Martin. *Fads and Fallacies in the Name of Science*. New York: New American Library, 1986 (reprint of 1952 edition). A classic look at pseudoscience by the master debunker. Includes sections of pseudoscientific beliefs in the 19th century.

Gonick, Larry, and Art Huffman. *The Cartoon Guide to Physics*. New York: Harper Perennial, 1991. Lively well-illustrated look at physics for young readers. Good, brief explanations of basic laws and short historical overviews accompany many easy experiments readers can perform.

Hazen, Robert M., and James Trefil. *Science Matters*. New York: Doubleday, 1991. A clear and readable overview of basic principles of science and how they apply to science in today's world.

Holzinger, Philip R. *The House of Science*. New York: John Wiley and Sons, 1990. Lively question-and-answer discussion of science for young adults. Includes activities and experiments.

Trefil, James. *1001 Things Everyone Should Know about Science*. New York, Doubleday, 1992. The subtitle, *Achieving Scientific Literacy*, tells all. Well done for the average reader but includes little history.

———. *The Nature of Science: An A–Z Guide to the Laws & Principles Governing Our Universe*. New York: Houghton Mifflin, 2003. An especially honest essay on the nature of science opens the book, followed by highly readable discussions of discoveries made in the fields of astronomy, chemistry, physics, and the life sciences. Simple charts indicate the historical relationship of related discoveries.

About the History of Nineteenth-Century Science

Brock, William H. *The Chemical Tree: A History of Chemistry.* Norton History of Science, Roy Porter, ed. New York: W. W. Norton and Co., 1993. Covers the work and discoveries of Dalton, Mendeleyev, and Kekulé.

Brooke, John Hedley. *Science and Religion: Some Historical Perspectives.* Cambridge: Cambridge University Press, 1991. Well-balanced and thoughtful look at the sometimes troubled relationship between science and religion.

Corben, Herbert C. *The Struggle to Understand: A History of Human Wonder and Discovery.* Buffalo, N.Y.: Prometheus Books, 1991. Explores the history of scientific discovery and superstition and supernaturalism from prehistoric times to the present.

Internet History of Science Sourcebook. Available online. URL: http://www.fordham.edu/halsall/science/sciencesbook.html. Accessed June 23, 2003.

Jones, Bessie Zaban, ed. *The Golden Age of Science: Thirty Portraits of the Giants of 19th-Century Science by Their Scientific Contemporaries.* New York: Simon and Schuster, 1966. A classic anthology of primary sources.

Mackay, Charles. *Extraordinary Popular Delusions and the Madness of Crowds.* New York: Harmony Books, 1990. Reprint of the classic 1841 book on various money-making schemes and outlandish beliefs people have bought into. Provides a fascinating sense of the time in which it was written as well as ageless insights into human psychology and its struggles against logic. Includes original illustrations and a present-day foreword by business writer Andrew Tobias.

Porter, Roy, ed. *The Cambridge Illustrated History of Medicine.* Cambridge, Mass.: Cambridge University Press, 2001. In essays written by experts in the field, this illustrated history traces the evolution of medicine from the contributions made by early Greek physicians through the Renaissance, Scientific Revolution, and 19th and 20th centuries up to current advances. Sidebars cover parallel social or political events and certain diseases.

Silver, Brian L. *The Ascent of Science.* New York: Oxford University Press, 1998. A sweeping overview of the history of science from the Renaissance to the present.

Timelinescience: One Thousand Years of Scientific Thought. National Grid for Learning (NGfL, British Educational Communications and Technology Agency). Available online. URL: http://www.timelinescience.org/index.php. Accessed June 23, 2003.

Victorian Science: An Overview. Available online. URL: http://65.107.211. 206/science/sciov.html. Accessed June 23, 2003.

About the Physical Sciences

Boorse, Henry A., Lloyd Motz, and Jefferson Hane Weaver. *The Atomic Scientists: A Biographical History.* New York: John Wiley and Son's, 1989. Includes a brief but informative chapter on Dalton, Gay-Lussac, and Avogadro. Concise and well written.

Gamow, George. *The Great Physicists from Galileo to Einstein.* New York: Dover Publications, Ind., 1988. Renowned physicist George Gamow takes a look at some major historical physicists and their work—highly readable and enlightening.

Hudson, John. *The History of Chemistry.* New York: Chapman and Hall, 1992. A highly readable account, including profiles on key scientists, photographs, and diagrams.

McCormmach, Russell. *Night Thoughts of a Classical Physicist.* Paperback. Cambridge: Harvard University Press, 1991. Set in Germany in the early days of the 20th century, this intriguing novel explores the mind and emotions of a physicist, trained in the approaches of 19th-century physics, who attempts to understand the disturbing changes in physics and the world.

Spielberg, Nathan, and Bryon D. Anderson. *Seven Ideas That Shook the Universe.* New York: John Wiley and Sons, 1987. Still readily available, this fascinating book centers on the drama of scientific discovery, including a thorough chapter on concepts of energy and entropy.

On Astronomers and Physicists

Buttmann, Günther. *The Shadow of the Telescope: A Biography of John Herschel.* Cambridge: Lutterworth Press, 2001. Entertaining look at the life and time of William Herschel's son, John, a famous astronomer and personality in his own right.

Cantor, Geoffrey, David Gooding, and Frank A. J. L. James. *Michael Faraday.* Paperback. Amherst, N.Y.: Humanity Books, 1996.

Cropper, William H. *Great Physicists: The Life and Times of Leading Physicists from Galileo to Hawking.* New York: Oxford University Press, 2003. Lively coverage of 19th-century contributors to thermodynamics (including Carnot, Mayer, Joule, and Helmhotz) and electromagnetism (Faraday and Maxwell).

Thomas, John Meurig. *Michael Faraday and the Royal Institution: The Genius of Man and Place.* Bristol: Adam Hilger (IOP Publishing, Ltd.), 1991. Written by the current director of the Royal Institution and the Davy Faraday Laboratory, this short, delightful study includes partial facsimiles of some of Faraday's manuscripts and photographs from the archives of the Royal Institution. Also covers the history of the Royal Institution.

On the Life Sciences, Darwin, and Evolution

Levine, Russell, and Chris Evers. The Slow Death of Spontaneous Generation. Access Excellence at the National Health Museum: About Biotech. Available online. URL: http://www.accessexcellence.org/AB/BC/Spontaneous_Generation.html. Accessed September 15, 2003.

Bowlby, John. *Charles Darwin: A New Life.* New York: W. W. Norton Company, 1990. Off-the-beaten-path look at Darwin, concerned chiefly with his mysterious medical problems. Worth a look but only after pursuing many other better books on the subject.

Bowler, Peter J. *Evolution: The History of an Idea.* Revised Edition. Berkeley, Calif.: University of California Press, 1989. An excellent look at the history of evolutionary theory. Includes many of the subjects included in this book. Highly thoughtful and informative.

Burkhardt, F., and S. Smith, eds. *The Correspondence of Charles Darwin,* 7 vols. Cambridge: Cambridge University Press, 1985–91. The definitive edition of Darwin's letters.

Darwin, Charles. *On the Origin of Species by Means of Natural Selection, or the Preservation of Favoured Races in the Struggle for Life* . . . London: Murray, 1859. Also available in many annotated and paperback additions.

———. *The Descent of Man and Selection in Relation to Sex,* 2 vols. London: Murray, 1871; 2nd ed. rev., 1874. Also available in annotated and paperback editions.

Desmond, Adrian, and James Moore. *Darwin.* New York: Warner Books, 1991. Desmond and Moore make use of much new material and offer a modern and updated look at Charles Darwin, his life, and work. Emphasizes the social and political background of Darwin's thought but sometimes tries to rewrite history in modern terms. Still the best modern book on Darwin.

Edey, Maitland, and Donald C. Johanson. *Blueprints: Solving the Mystery of Evolution.* Boston: Little, Brown and Co., 1989. Engrossingly told story, coauthored by paleoanthropologist Johanson, the discoverer of the famous "Lucy."

Eldredge, Niels. *The Monkey Business: A Scientist Looks at Creationism.* New York: Washington Square Press, 1982. A top evolutionary scientist answers the creationists' attack on evolutionary theory.

The Huxley File. Available online. URL: http://aleph0.clarku.edu/huxley/. Accessed June 23, 2003.

Jastrow, Robert, and Kenneth Korey. *The Essential Darwin.* Boston: Little, Brown and Company, 1984. An invaluable primary source: readings from Darwin with editorial comments and explanations by Jastrow and Korey.

Keynes, Randal. *Darwin, His Daughter, and Human Evolution.* New York: Riverhead Books, 2002. An examination of Darwin's beliefs and scientific integrity in the face of the death of his beloved daughter Annie; written by Darwin's great-great-grandson and based on notes Darwin made during his daughter's illness.

Mayr, Ernst. *One Long Argument: Charles Darwin and the Genesis of Modern Evolutionary Thought.* Cambridge, Mass.: Harvard University Press, 1991.

McGowan, Chris. *In The Beginning: A Scientist Shows Why the Creationists Are Wrong.* Buffalo: Prometheus Books, 1984. In this classic, still readily available book, a scientist offers insights for students or anyone wishing to understand more about the still-heated evolution versus creationist debate. McGowan's book offers a reasoned attack against the creationist arguments.

Milner, Richard. *The Encyclopedia of Evolution: Humanity's Search for Its Origins.* New York: Facts On File, 1990. Totally engrossing for hunting facts or browsing, one of the few books of its kind that is also completely rewarding, entertaining, and informative as just plain reading. Quirky and fascinating and chock-full of just about everything you wanted to know about evolution but were afraid to ask.

Morris, Richard. *The Evolutionists: The Struggle for Darwin's Soul.* New York: W. H. Freeman and Company, 2001. Contains good descriptions of Darwinism and Darwin's development of evolutionary theory, as well as discussions of 21st-century views spearheaded by Richard Dawkins and Stephen Jay Gould.

Reader, John. *Missing Links: The Hunt for Earliest Man.* Boston: Little, Brown and Company, 1981. The hunt for the so-called "missing link" between ape and human that began with the discovery of the first Neandertal skeleton in 1856.

Trinkaus, Erik, and Pat Shipman. *The Neandertals: Changing the Image of Mankind.* New York: Alfred A. Knopf, 1993. Just about the latest and most up-to-date information on the new light being shed on the once poorly understood Neandertals. A good, solid book, nicely researched, but a little difficult to read.

Wallace, David Rains. *The Bonehunters' Revenge: Dinosaurs, Greed, and the Greatest Scientific Feud of the Gilded Age.* New York: Houghton Mifflin Co., 1999. A fast-paced examination of the great battle between Marsh and Cope, widely considered the definitive account.

Zimmer, Carl. *Evolution: The Triumph of an Idea.* Companion to the PBS Series. Introduction by Stephen Jay Gould. Foreword by Richard Hutton. New York: HarperCollins Publishers, 2001.

Periodic Table of Elements

Legend:

1	atomic number
H	atomic number
1.008	atomic weight

Numbers in parentheses are the atomic mass numbers of radioactive isotopes.

1	2	3	4	5	6	7	8	9	10	11	12	13	14	15	16	17	18
1 H 1.008																	2 He 4.003
3 Li 6.941	4 Be 9.012											5 B 10.81	6 C 12.01	7 N 14.01	8 O 16.00	9 F 19.00	10 Ne 20.18
11 Na 22.99	12 Mg 24.31											13 Al 26.98	14 Si 28.09	15 P 30.97	16 S 32.07	17 Cl 35.45	18 Ar 39.95
19 K 39.10	20 Ca 40.08	21 Sc 44.96	22 Ti 47.88	23 V 50.94	24 Cr 52.00	25 Mn 54.94	26 Fe 55.85	27 Co 58.93	28 Ni 58.69	29 Cu 63.55	30 Zn 65.39	31 Ga 69.72	32 Ge 72.59	33 As 74.92	34 Se 78.96	35 Br 79.90	36 Kr 83.80
37 Rb 85.47	38 Sr 87.62	39 Y 88.91	40 Zr 91.22	41 Nb 92.91	42 Mo 95.94	43 Tc (98)	44 Ru 101.1	45 Rh 102.9	46 Pd 106.4	47 Ag 107.9	48 Cd 112.4	49 In 114.8	50 Sn 118.7	51 Sb 121.8	52 Te 127.6	53 I 126.9	54 Xe 131.3
55 Cs 132.9	56 Ba 137.3	57-71*	72 Hf 178.5	73 Ta 180.9	74 W 183.9	75 Re 186.2	76 Os 190.2	77 Ir 192.2	78 Pt 195.1	79 Au 197.0	80 Hg 200.6	81 Tl 204.4	82 Pb 207.2	83 Bi 209.0	84 Po (210)	85 At (210)	86 Rn (222)
87 Fr (223)	88 Ra (226)	89-103‡	104 Rf (261)	105 Db (262)	106 Sg (263)	107 Bh (262)	108 Hs (265)	109 Mt (266)	110 Ds (271)	111 Uuu (272)	112 Uub (285)	113 Uut (284)	114 Uuq (289)	115 Uup (288)			

*lanthanide series

57 La 138.9	58 Ce 140.1	59 Pr 140.9	60 Nd 144.2	61 Pm (145)	62 Sm 150.4	63 Eu 152.0	64 Gd 157.3	65 Tb 158.9	66 Dy 162.5	67 Ho 164.9	68 Er 167.3	69 Tm 168.9	70 Yb 173.0	71 Lu 175.0

‡actinide series

89 Ac (227)	90 Th 232.0	91 Pa 231.0	92 U 238.0	93 Np (237)	94 Pu (244)	95 Am (243)	96 Cm (247)	97 Bk (247)	98 Cf (251)	99 Es (252)	100 Fm (257)	101 Md (258)	102 No (259)	103 Lr (260)

The periodic table as it looks today

The Chemical Elements

element	symbol	a.n.	element	symbol	a.n.	element	symbol	a.n.	element	symbol	a.n.
actinium	Ac	89	erbium	Er	68	molybdenum	Mo	42	selenium	Se	34
aluminum	Al	13	europium	Eu	63	neodymium	Nd	60	silicon	Si	14
americium	Am	95	fermium	Fm	100	neon	Ne	10	silver	Ag	47
antimony	Sb	51	fluorine	F	9	neptunium	Np	93	sodium	Na	11
argon	Ar	18	francium	Fr	87	nickel	Ni	28	strontium	Sr	38
arsenic	As	33	gadolinium	Gd	64	niobium	Nb	41	sulfur	S	16
astatine	At	85	gallium	Ga	31	nitrogen	N	7	tantalum	Ta	73
barium	Ba	56	germanium	Ge	32	nobelium	No	102	technetium	Tc	43
berkelium	Bk	97	gold	Au	79	osmium	Os	76	tellurium	Te	52
beryllium	Be	4	hafnium	Hf	72	oxygen	O	8	terbium	Tb	65
bismuth	Bi	83	hassium	Hs	108	palladium	Pd	46	thallium	Tl	81
bohrium	Bh	107	helium	He	2	phosphorus	P	15	thorium	Th	90
boron	B	5	holmium	Ho	67	platinum	Pt	78	thulium	Tm	69
bromine	Br	35	hydrogen	H	1	plutonium	Pu	94	tin	Sn	50
cadmium	Cd	48	indium	In	49	polonium	Po	84	titanium	Ti	22
calcium	Ca	20	iodine	I	53	potassium	K	19	tungsten	W	74
californium	Cf	98	iridium	Ir	77	praseodymium	Pr	59	ununbium	Uub	112
carbon	C	6	iron	Fe	26	promethium	Pm	61	ununpentium	Uup	115
cerium	Ce	58	krypton	Kr	36	protactinium	Pa	91	ununquadium	Uuq	114
cesium	Cs	55	lanthanum	La	57	radium	Ra	88	ununtrium	Uut	113
chlorine	Cl	17	lawrencium	Lr	103	radon	Rn	86	unununium	Uuu	111
chromium	Cr	24	lead	Pb	82	rhenium	Re	75	uranium	U	92
cobalt	Co	27	lithium	Li	3	rhodium	Rh	45	vanadium	V	23
copper	Cu	29	lutetium	Lu	71	rubidium	Rb	37	xenon	Xe	54
curium	Cm	96	magnesium	Mg	12	ruthenium	Ru	44	ytterbium	Yb	70
darmstadtium	Ds	110	manganese	Mn	25	rutherfordium	Rf	104	yttrium	Y	39
dubnium	Db	105	meitnerium	Mt	109	samarium	Sm	62	zinc	Zn	30
dysprosium	Dy	66	mendelevium	Md	101	scandium	Sc	21	zirconium	Zr	40
einsteinium	Es	99	mercury	Hg	80	seaborgium	Sg	106			

a.n. = atomic number

INDEX